Come On In, There's Room For Us All

June 05

To Carolyn —
When women join hands, all things are possible!

♡ Ginger

HOW NETWORKING STARTED IN SAN ANTONIO: This photo appeared in the *San Antonio Express-News*, February 15, 1981. It shows representatives of the eight women's groups Ginger Purdy brought together to bring the concept of Networking to San Antonio. Left to right: Roseanna Szliak, YWCA; Latrell Johnson, National Association of Negro Business and Professional Women's Clubs; Vangie Aguilera, Mexican-American Business and Professional Women; Helen Butler, Women in Business; Carole Bufler, American Association of University Women; Ginger Purdy, Women in Communications, Inc.; Kay Moore, Women's Opportunity Workshops, San Antonio College; and Yvonne Hansen, Bexar County Women's Center.

Come On In, There's Room For Us All

Finding Your Place in the Women's Movement

Finally! The middle woman speaks up & out!

Ginger Purdy

San Antonio
1996

Copyright © Ginger Purdy 1996

All rights reserved. Printed in the U.S.A.

First Edition

A *Watercress Press Book* from
Evett & Associates, San Antonio, Texas

Cover and book design by Mary Fletcher-Owens

Additional copies may be ordered from
The Middle Woman
P. O. Box 17591, San Antonio, Texas 78217-8162

Library of Congress Catalog Card No. 96-60296
ISBN 0-934955-30-1

Dedication

*To my mother, Mary,
and my five daughters,
Mary, Melissa, Martha,
Janet, and Alison*

This book is published in loving memory of
Billie Vaughan,
also known as Mattie Evelyn Badelia Zeiger Hay,
grandmother of Patricia Harding Smothers

A Lifetime Advocate for Women

Acknowledgements

Like everything in my life including this book, I would be back on square one if it weren't for the good people who have been there for me along the way. So I salute them all!

I do have to give special thanks to my daughters: To Martha, the youngest, who put in long hours at the computer. And Melissa, the middle one and the real writer, who lent her editorial skills. And to Mary, the eldest, a graphic designer of great talent, as evidenced by this book's cover and inside art and design. And to my stepdaughters, Janet and Alison, who have supported me every step of the way.

Jan Kilby, Ph.D., was the driving force that got everything started, and my publisher, Alice Evett, whose path first crossed mine thirty years ago in another life, got it all finished. I have been truly blessed to have such help and support.

San Antonio, Texas
February 4, 1996

Ginger Purdy

Contents

Foreword by Ann Richards ... ix

Part One What in the World is the Middle Woman? ... 1
  1 Introduction ... 3
  2 Why We Must Network ... 5

Part Two This is My Story: The Miracle of Middle Women ... 7
  3 Early Childhood and Home Life ... 8
  4 The College Years ... 15
  5 First Marriage ... 19
  6 Learning to Speak: Fear and the Fish-Pond Booth ... 26

Part Three The Single Years: Counting to Ten Backwards ... 29
  7 My New Baby ... 30
  8 Firing My Monster God ... 37
  9 This Pedestal Business ... 41

Part Four Coming Out in the Open: Creating the Philosophy of the Middle Woman ... 47
  10 Second Marriage: The Good, the Bad, and the Unbelievable ... 48
  11 Hooked on Helping through Pro Bono Public Relations ... 54
  12 "Ginny, I Love You" ... 57
  13 Who ... Me? ... A Leader? ... 60
  14 President of WICI in San Antonio ... 65
  15 "Ginger Purdy and Daughters" ... 67
  16 Still Scared but Speaking Out: "Network Power/Texas" is Born ... 70

Part Five Going National with the Middle Woman Philosophy ... 77
  17 "Good Morning America" ... 78
  18 Creativity Takes Off: Founding Two Organizations ... 81

19	"Can Networking Do Anything for a Woman Like Me?"	87
20	The Late Bloomer: From Follower to Leader	91
21	The Ego Trip: Suffering the Slings of Others to Stand Up for Yourself	94
22	Courage	99
23	"Women's Legislative Days"	109
24	Lessons from "Dear Abby": Using All of One's Communication Skills to Spread the Message	112
Part Six	The Making of a Middle Woman	115
25	Learning to Take Care of Myself	116
26	Shirley Chisholm: Women Speaking with One Voice — "Organize and Strategize"	119
27	The Network Power/Texas Seminar and the Commitment Lesson	122
28	The Pay Equity Campaign	125
29	Founding the San Antonio Women's Chamber of Commerce	128
Part Seven	Political Awareness Pays Off	133
30	Founding "Ann's Fans"	134
31	"W6" — Bound with Butter	138
32	Networking with International Women	141
33	The University of Texas at San Antonio's Women's Center	144
34	Networking in Mexico	146
35	Becoming a Full-Time Women's Advocate	151
Part Eight	Make My Challenge Your Challenge!	155
36	Powerful Women Who Have Touched My Life	156
37	Follow me to Freedom!	161

Coda	172
Works Cited	183
Index	189
About the Author	195

Foreword

In many ways my life is an example of what can happen as women begin to more fully realize their potential. Like other women of my generation, our lives revolved around our families and home life. Seeing the ways our families and communities were affected by the decisions made for us by elected officials, we understood that we had to take a larger role in determining our future. Many of us became politically active over issues that especially concerned our children. Others worked on changing the inequities in the laws governing divorce settlements, home-ownership, and property rights. Further activism gave rise to the legal recognition of financial contributions made by traditional homemakers for the first time. Many women were able to get credit in their own names for the first time. As their foremothers before them, women renewed their efforts to obtain civil rights and equality for all.

Taking responsibility for our own lives not only led to further political involvement but provided the enhancement of our sense of self-esteem and self-reliance. As I tell young women, this is the foundation for a full and satisfying life.

Women must speak out. No one else can do it for us. You must exercise your right to vote. And vote only for those who respect and support your rights. Your independence is the best gift you can give yourself.

Ginger Purdy and I met years ago through our membership in the Women's Political Caucus. Ginger's life is also the story of how a woman becomes politically active. Her rallying cry has been, "If I can do it, any woman can!"

Attending the United Nation's 4th World Conference on Women in Beijing, China, in the fall of 1995 enabled Ginger to experience firsthand the women of the world uniting, as never before, to work for women's rights as human rights. This was the largest conference ever held on the planet. It was also further proof of the "maturing" of the women's movement: women realizing that they must speak with one voice on every issue that concerns their well-being.

To every woman who reads this book, follow Ginger's advice: Take charge of your own life. The miracles that happen will be the ones you bring about yourself. It's up to you to create your own future. Involvement in working towards women's equality is an important way to begin. You have nothing to lose and a rich and rewarding life to gain. So "Come On In, There's Room For Us All!"

Austin, Texas *Ann Richards*
February 18, 1996

Come On In, There's Room For Us All

Part One

What in the World is the Middle Woman?

Chapter 1
Introduction

For many reasons that must be respected, there are countless numbers of women who have not been able to identify with the extremists at either end of the women's movement, a movement that some sociologists have suggested may be the most significant revolution in the history of humankind. It is one that has had a lasting effect on the way people relate to each other in their personal and professional lives.

So it has to be something of a miracle that it took a man to help a woman discover who she was and the part she could play in marshalling more women to join in the movement toward equality.

What is a Middle Woman and how did I come to use this term to describe myself? This is where my second husband comes in for the credit. When I told him in 1980 of my concerns about not being able to relate to the extremists, he asked me to perform an experiment that changed my life forever. He asked me to draw a continuum (a simple line, to those of us who are not scientists) representing the women's movement, with the extremists at either end—from the militant, man-hating types at one end to the duplicitous-sounding anti-feminists at the other. Then he asked me where I would fit on that line.

I looked at him and said, "Honey, I'd be right in the middle!"

So he said what has proved to be very prophetic to me. "Okay, Ginger. You go ahead and speak out as the 'Middle Woman.' Your voice has just as much right to be heard as anyone else's."

In my lectures, I always spell out clearly what a "Middle Woman" is. She is a woman who loves being a woman, loves men, and believes that the family is the basic unit of society. She loves being a wife and a mother, but she also loves developing and using the other talents she has been given.

The Middle Woman believes that husband and wife meet to share their responsibilities as equal human beings and that if a woman chooses to work outside the home, whether it is in the office, on the assembly line, or in the boardroom, she should be paid equally on an equal level with men. This, in essence, is a "Middle Woman." It has nothing to do with middle age or mediocrity. It has everything to do with fairness, freedom, and justice.

Why did I finally decide to go public with my "Middle Woman" philosophy? As Paul Tillich said, "Decision is a risk rooted in the courage of being free." The joy and freedom I've attained by having the courage to take the risk to be myself is the joy and freedom I want for all my sisters. This is my gift to them.

Chapter 2
Why We Must Network

My networking mentor, Alina Novak, one of the early pioneers in women's networking, once used the analogy of Sleeping Beauty to demonstrate why we must network. Sleeping Beauty slept for one hundred years, and someone else, the prince, had to wake her up. We don't have that kind of time; we have to wake ourselves up. Believe me, networking is what will do it for us. Even though for the last dozen years or so networking has become a relatively new name for an old process, it is what has enabled women to come together to talk about how to help themselves by helping each other.

When I first started on my networking speaking career, most of my audience was female. I gradually noticed more men in attendance. Of course, when they heard me start to speak, their arms were often folded across their chests. They would not give me eye contact but looked, instead, at my right or left earlobe. I'm sure they were thinking, "Oh no, another raging, militant, man-hating feminist." However, as they heard my story and my mission to help women, they relaxed their arms and looked me straight in the eye. (If you want to reach men when talking about women's issues, you can't do it by relating to their wives. You get them every time by talking about their daughters! Daddy wants his little girl to have everything everyone else has.)

We must network to be informed about what is going on in the workplace and in the community. We must network against a male-dominated system that excludes us from decision-making and power. We must network for better paying jobs; you hear about such jobs through people.

Networking is the dissemination of information, and information is power. We must network to change the system that tries to keep women second-class citizens. We must network to increase our self-esteem, self-confidence, assertiveness, and personal power.

I know there are many who think that networking is now old hat. What they fail to realize is how long it takes for those who really need it to find out about it!

In the last fifteen years, I have seen it happen over and over again: Through networking, women have created their own personal power base. This is something that no one can take away from them. It is the most gratifying feeling in the world to see a disadvantaged minority woman find herself and her personal power base through networking. What is even better is to have played a part in her awakening.

Yes, networking is what we have always done at the backyard fence, at the church social, and at the coffee klatch, but we didn't have a name for it then. We did it for everything and everyone but ourselves.

This has all changed now, and it will be changing even more when the "Middle Women" come together to speak with one voice. Halleluja!

Part Two

This is My Story:
The Miracle of Middle Women

Chapter 3
Early Childhood and Home Life

Once upon a time, there was a little girl who grew up with a huge inferiority complex. She had no sense of self-worth or personhood. She felt that she was a non-person. In later life, her mother assured her that she grew up with love in a loving family. She was the eldest child and had a younger sister and a brother, a mother at home, and a father at work. In spite of what her mother said, she knew that she had not received the emotional support that she needed to have a sense of her own self-worth.

She thought that everyone was smarter than she was (even though she had an extremely high IQ), everyone was better looking than she was (even though she had been called "beautiful"), and that everyone else's family had more material wealth than hers (hers was an average, middle-class family). Not only did she have an inferiority complex, but she also grew up with a large shame core, a common occurrence in dysfunctional families. There was an almost overwhelming sense that she and her family did not quite measure up, that surely they were second class!

All of her life if she thought of herself at all it was in the role of a follower. She was a very hard worker and totally dependable. One of her most acute memories was of her second-grade teacher, Miss Levy, telling the class as Virginia

Early Childhood and Home Life

returned to the room from doing an errand for her, "Virginia White is very dependable. If you ask her to do something, she will do it without fail." This one instance of verbal affirmation set in motion a lifelong sense of responsibility that was always carried to the extreme. She would rather die than fail to carry out a promised commitment, no matter how difficult it was or how indisposed she was at the moment.

This little girl was me. In later life, after I was on the road to recovery, I admitted to myself that I was the adult child of an alcoholic, coming from a family that was dysfunctional on both sides . . . and probably had been for generations. I was a co-dependent of the first order and my family was the classic alcoholic one . . . characterized by denial in the extreme.

Two events occurred in my life almost simultaneously that brought about my acknowledgement that I was a late bloomer, but thank God I did bloom! The first by several years, 1978, was my introduction into the Al-Anon program. The second, 1980, was my commitment to the concept of networking to change followers into leaders and losers into winners and helping people become the leaders and winners in their own lives.

What is making me so successful in my mission to free up "Middle Women" is that I have overcome every downer that holds women back from self-actualization, self-fulfillment, and self-confidence. My rallying cry is, "If I can do it, any woman can!"

I have been fortunate to have the most amazing woman in the world as a mother. Even today, at ninety, she is absolutely ageless — full of love and with an outlook on life as fresh and eager as a sixteen-year-old. It has always been so meaningful to me that after her three children reached the age of consent she always treated us as adults.

She definitely had a life of her own, even though she never worked outside her home throughout her marriage.

I always had the feeling that she was ready to listen to anything you wanted to share with her, but she never imposed her views or judgments. It's a wonderful feeling to know that someone you love deeply is always there for you, no matter what.

My mother has been a widow since 1974. Since I am her only offspring in the same city, I make it a point to call her once each day, usually around noon, to make sure she's okay. Now, I say that, but, in reality, I'm the one who benefits from the phone call. Just to hear her cheery voice is a mood-lifter. When I ask the question, "What are you doing?" she always has an answer and it's usually "I'm busy," doing something around the house or in the kitchen. My mother is always busy.

Mama is a living, breathing encyclopedia about literally everything in this world. She knows what's going on worldwide, whether it's current events, sporting or entertainment events, or the everyday chitchat in the community life. Because I am my mother's daughter, a busy go-go, I can call her at any time of the day to find out the news. All of the major events that happen in the world I usually hear about from my mother long before I turn on the evening news.

Mama is a sports fan supreme. I love to watch sporting events with her. My only brother is a natural athlete who started sports in grade school. The group of young boys he grew up with played all the sports—football, basketball, baseball, and track—throughout all their school years. Brother Ben was an all-state in high school and then went on to college with an athletic scholarship, Mama encouraging him all the way. He was even drafted by a professional football team after graduation, but a knee injury ended his professional football career. So we really were a sports family.

One of the reasons why I feel Mama was such a positive influence on my brother in encouraging him and his friends to pursue sports was that it taught them good sportsmanship. Throughout all their years together, there never was any kind of trouble from their behavior.

Early Childhood and Home Life

We all love to watch sports on TV with Mama. She knows all the coaches and all the players, and she can usually tell you what play they should have run. Oh yes, I forgot one sport — she also follows golf!

I don't know how popular the game of Bunco is today, but my mother has belonged to the same Bunco Club for at least the last sixty years. They call themselves "the girls," and some of them even attended high school together. I think it is truly amazing and a tribute to my mother's ability to make friends and to keep friends that this club has existed for so long. They used to entertain in their homes. However, since they've gotten older, they often eat at restaurants and then return to their hostess's home for the Bunco game. Some of my fondest memories were sitting in as a substitute at Mama's Bunco Club. You really had to watch your P's and Q's because you could easily lose a finger if you threw a Bunco and failed to grab it quickly.

Even though I have always had such a close and loving relationship with my mother everything didn't always go smoothly. A perfect example of this is what I call the "anger episode." Because I had always been a quiet and shy child, I was never overtly angry with my mother ... or so I thought. Years later, in my adult life, when I was in counseling for co-dependency, the counselor asked if I had any anger toward my mother that I needed to confront. The answer was, "Oh no, I just love my mother more than anything in the world."

But after I had dealt with some personal issues in the course of doing a fourth step in my Al-Anon program several years later, it occurred to me that perhaps I *had* been harboring some childhood anger toward my mother. I went back to the counselor to say that I wanted to deal with that subject, and the counselor threw back her head, gave a good laugh, and said, "I knew from the very beginning that you had some anger issues that you needed to deal with concerning your mother."

One of my painful childhood memories was sitting with my brother and sister in the backseat of our big Packard touring car. My mother was sitting patiently behind the wheel, waiting for my father to come out of his office. He would be inside drinking with some of his buddies, and to my child's mind it seemed as if we waited for hours and hours. I can remember being tired and hungry and crying that I wanted to go home. My mother would say, "It's alright; he'll be out in a little while," and we would continue to wait. All that anger that I felt toward my mother was stuffed. After all, nice little girls didn't get mad at their parents.

In counseling, when I was involved with some in-depth study on my road to self-discovery, I remarked to my small support group that because I was the Little Miss Goody-Two-Shoes in the family, I never rebelled like most teenagers. Much to my surprise, I learned that I had indeed rebelled, but in a sly, sneaky way. Because my mother was a very punctual woman, always arriving early for an event, guess what her daughter did? I have been continually late to everything all my life, not late-late, but just several minutes late, enough to disturb my serenity and cause me anxiety. It was pointed out to me that this was probably the way I had dealt with my anger toward my mother.

I will never forget the feelings I experienced with realization that my habitual lateness was a way of getting back at Mama. After I had worked through all of the ramifications, I went to her to share all of this. It was a tremendous relief to get it all out in the open. We put our arms around each other and forgave each other. She shared with me that down through the years she had always felt guilty about making her children wait when she should have taken them home and let her husband get home the best that he could.

Our sharing was a very joyful experience, and we had a good laugh over her daughter's habitual lateness. I am getting better about being on time, but a lifetime habit is not easy to break. At least I'm working on it.

My mother is one of the greatest "people persons" I've known in my life. Our home was always a safe haven for anyone in need. Probably Mama was known as a "soft touch," but she was the most loved woman all of us had ever known.

Her father, Grandpa Reno, had been the last blacksmith in a small town in the Texas Hill Country. Grandpa had never owned a car; he didn't trust them. I can remember that when Mama drove our car, Grandpa sat in the back, behind her, with the door open and his foot on the running board so he could jump in case of an accident. He was truly from the horse-and-buggy days.

When Grandpa wanted to come visit Mama, he would hitch a ride with whichever farm family was coming to the big city. It might be a farmer and his wife with a dozen children, but he would always say the same words, "We'll go to Mary's for lunch." It never fazed my mother. She could put a meal on the table faster than anyone I've ever seen. I don't know how she did it, but there always seemed to be enough food, and she always kept her good humor. Anyone else would have told Grandpa where to go, but not Mama. She made everyone feel welcome.

I think the world would be a much better place if there were more people like my mother running things. Mama operates her life strictly from the love point of view. It doesn't matter who you are or what your skin color or nationality is. Everyone receives Mama's love.

I remember one Sunday in church when a young man in the pew directly in front of us went into an epileptic seizure. All of the people jumped up in fear to move away from the scene, but not Mama! She never changed her kneeling stance but quickly reached over to gather the young man in her arms, holding him against her shoulder to keep him from injuring himself. She did this until the seizure passed. Even as a child, I was in awe of the love and respect she had for all who came her way.

I know that I have been given an unbelievable gift from this truly amazing woman. In all of the work that I do today as a women's advocate, I am continually told about my ability to motivate people and about my physical energy. I realize that these are gifts I have received from my mother, and

I never fail to let people know where I got them. Dutch author Corrie TenBoom had a lovely way of expressing how she handled compliments. She said she would gather each one like a beautiful flower and then, at the end of each day, she would offer the bouquet up to her God in thanksgiving, because that's the source of all gifts. I give thanks to my God for my mother.

Chapter 4
The College Years

Education was important in my family, but because of financial circumstances, that option had not been open to all of us. My father's father had graduated from the Episcopal Seminary in Virginia, then came West to visit his sister and became a cattleman instead of a minister.

Daddy was the smartest man I've ever known. His father had died at an early age of adult onset diabetes that passes on through the paternal side of the family. As a result, my father had to leave school with his education barely begun — as the eldest son in a family of six siblings he had to go to work to help his mother rear the children. His first job was delivering bread for $3 a week.

My father was a self-taught miracle. He was a whiz at math and anything that pertained to the analytical process. As a notary public, a position he held for most of his adult life, he was well versed in legal and ethical matters. I remember that when he helped me with my homework, particularly math, he would always arrive at the correct answer while I was still stumbling around. I was amazed at how he was able to do this.

Daddy was a giant of a man. He was tall — over six feet, four inches — and had a distinguished manner in his look and actions. His deep baritone voice commanded attention. Even though he never spanked me, his stern "Virginia Nan" pulled me back in line in a second.

He was an elegant dresser, always having the finest of clothes and was precise in the care of his personal hygiene and clothing. He had a great sense of trust and dignity about himself. He was the most principled of men. Strict about decorum and behavior, he never allowed anyone to use rude and profane language around his family.

I thought my father was wonderful. While I respected him greatly, I also feared him mightily. I'm sure that fear came from nothing more than his commanding presence. One of the saddest aspects of my life was that my father never told me he loved me. When he used to come home from work in the evenings, he would always greet me with a "Hello, little girl" and a pinch on my cheek. I know within my heart that he meant this as a loving greeting; however, someone of his size and strength did not realize that the cheerful pinch caused a great deal of pain to the receiver. I can remember my cheek being numb for quite a while after that greeting!

In later years, when I talked to my mother about the lack of emotional sharing with my father, she said, "Ginger, I know your father loved you with all his heart. He was just never able to voice it." That is one of the great tragedies of a dysfunctional family. The love is there, but the true feelings are never expressed.

I think I was the first in my immediate family to go away to college. It was important to my father that I had this opportunity, and I'm sure it took no little financial sacrifice to make it happen. Even though he never said so, I know he was tremendously proud of me when I received my college diploma.

I spent my freshman and sophomore years at Texas Women's University (TWU) in Denton, then the largest residential women's university in the country. I loved going to a women's college and was sorry years later that I could not talk any of my daughters into doing likewise.

The summer before my junior year in 1946, Daddy became seriously ill with diabetes. It was decided that I should continue my art major closer to home, so I enrolled at Trinity University in San Antonio three days after registration had closed. I guess special circumstances bring about special considerations—I was lucky in that all of my credits and classes transferred. I was somewhat overwhelmed to be among so many male students after two years at TWU besides being rather shy around the opposite sex.

Several weeks into the first semester, I was in a life drawing class one day when I had the strangest feeling that I was being watched. I glanced around but did not see anyone looking in my direction. The same feeling came the next time I was in that class. We all stood or sat before our easels that held large drawing pads.

Eventually I saw what was giving me the strange feeling of being watched. A darkly handsome young man had folded the cover of his drawing pad back over his easel, thus creating a sort of telescope that he had trained on me. I felt myself blushing as I realized he had probably been doing this at each class meeting.

What I noticed about my fellow art student was that he seemed to be some years older than the other men in the class. During our courtship, I found out that he was a returning veteran and was going to college on the GI Bill. What I didn't know until later was that he was only auditing the classes instead of taking them for credit. This lack of effort caused by fear or laziness should have tipped me off to a basic character flaw that would prove disastrous in our later life, but Jack was handsome, charming, and funny, and I found myself being captured by his romantic interest in me.

I did well my junior year at Trinity but had planned to return to TWU for my senior year because my father's condition had stabilized. Unfortunately, when I made plans to transfer back, I found that I would have to take several courses in my major that had not been available at Trinity. What this meant was that after I had spent a long term and a complete summer term at Trinity, I had to spend another long term and a summer term to graduate from TWU in August 1948.

By the time I graduated from TWU, I had amassed enough hours and grade points to earn two degrees, a Bachelor of Arts degree with a major in costume design and a Bachelor of Science degree with a major in fashion illustration, with minors in history and government. I remember that there were six of us in my graduating class who had these dual degrees.

When I headed back north to TWU, Jack went even further north to the Art Students' League in New York City. Our romance was carried on by phone and mail. By then I had already received an engagement ring and we were planning to be married after graduation. We were two young artists, both from severely dysfunctional families, without a care in the world, except the wonderful infatuation of being in love. Innocence is bliss!

Chapter 5
First Marriage

I was not aware at the time that I was, even then, a role model for women of my generation because I started my career immediately after graduating from college in 1948. Most women in my generation became housewives. Of course, I did exactly as my peers did, marrying within several weeks of college graduation from Texas Women's University. Jack was five years my senior, and we had been engaged for a year and a half.

In 1948, I was hired as a trainee fashion illustrator for Frank Brothers, a small San Antonio specialty department store for men with a women's sportswear department, thus fulfilling my goal since junior high school to be a fashion artist. I had listened to my Jefferson High School art teacher, Ms. Dugosh, and had graduated from a state-supported college that was well known for its diversified art majors.

For a while, I contemplated a career as a costume designer, one of my great loves, until I discovered that without a source of personal income, one could spend years in a back room designing under another's name and label. So I chose the field of fashion illustration.

I was fortunate to be hired by a small exclusive store with an outstanding reputation for dedicated service where I was allowed to develop in all areas of the retail advertising field, thus preparing me for a career in advertising management. After the first year, I was offered the job of advertising manager with a staff of three, one of whom had been a high school friend. For the next five years, I honed my skills and developed my ability to work with people under relentless deadlines and pressure.

When we were first married, Jack had an art studio that was connected to our home so he spent a great deal of time out there. He was one of the most fantastic artists I have ever known. He also had quite a sense of humor. For example, one Saturday morning when I had the rare opportunity to sleep in, he came into our bedroom, woke me up, and said he had something to do that required my help. In his hand was a cigar box filled with white plaster. He said, "Please sit up and take your nightgown strap down." Being barely awake, I did not know what he was talking about. I thought that since he was in a phase in his artistic life that concerned collages, he must need some new form.

I was right! He said, "I have a place on my collage that needs a little round thing." What he wanted was a plaster cast of one of my breasts. I told him, "No," in no uncertain terms. I thought he was crazy. Apparently, in his way-out view, it made good sense. My Saturday morning sleep was ruined by this episode. Later I could look back on it and laugh.

In 1954, after six years, I resigned my job to have my first child, working almost up to the delivery date, which was three weeks early. In those days, most women were terminated from their jobs when their pregnancy became obvious. The only reason I was allowed to work throughout my pregnancy was because I was in an advertising office away from the public.

A pregnancy at the end of my first year of marriage in 1948 had been terminated at the insistence of my husband who suddenly declared that he did not want children. He took me to Houston for an illegal abortion. The guilt from that decision, in addition to the guilt I carried from my initiation into Roman Catholicism at the age of twelve, contributed

First Marriage

to a sense of remorse that was almost unbearable, a feeling that I suffered in silence for almost half my life.

While I was pregnant with my first child, whom I desperately wanted, I suffered many indignities. Jack still insisted he did not want children. When I finally had the courage to tell him I was pregnant, he insisted the child was not his, even though I had never given him any reason to think otherwise. He slammed out the door and did not speak to me again for two weeks.

I never knew what to expect from him throughout my pregnancy. When friends asked him what he wanted, meaning a boy or a girl, he answered, "art supplies." He seemed to take perverse delight in commenting negatively about my increasing girth, one time bringing me to tears by saying that I looked like a fat frog as I sat painting the baby's crib.

While I was pregnant, we were also in the throes of building a home. We went through the agony of having our dream house designed by an architect friend, only to have the cost estimate come in many thousands of dollars over our budget. We had to abandon almost a year of work to start over and we finally settled on a stock house plan that, with some alternations, could become acceptable, but it was not nearly as elegantly modern as our first choice.

We moved in two months before the birth of Mary, our first daughter. Jack's only outward show of emotion after the birth was an arrangement of flowers with a note that read, "Good show, old girl."

I loved being a mother and said later that if I could have had the right kind of husband I would have had a passel of children because I loved taking care of tiny babies. My strong maternal instinct led me to nurse all of my children, the first for almost a year.

I kept up my career from 1954 to 1967 while being a mother through my work as a home-based freelance artist. Some of my clients included the Guarantee Shoe Company, Joske's of Texas, and Sears.

A second daughter, Melissa, was born in 1958, almost five

years after the first one. Again I went through the indignity of being told my baby was not my husband's child. The second child was the closest in family resemblance to her father, and he pronounced her his favorite, but without any real show of emotion.

I continued my freelance work, being lucky to have extremely loyal clients. This flex-time work enabled me to be a full-time mother while producing fashion art. The added income allowed me to give my daughters swimming and dancing lessons.

During this time, my main role was trying to maintain a semblance of a normal marriage and family life, while living with a volatile-tempered artist. A counselor later told me that he could not understand why Jack's parents had not dragged him into treatment by the time he was twenty-one. My continual concern was keeping the peace between my children and me and my erratic husband.

Fortunately, he was seldom at home, being either at work or, after work, at the art studio he rented. When he was home I was nervous, since his rage could erupt at any time or at anything. I once saw him throw a swing-set over the backyard fence because our oldest child had hurt herself on it. Another time I retreated to the bathroom to escape his wrath, only to have him put his fist through the hallway wall.

At that time, I was not aware of the emotional damage this kind of life was doing to my children and me. Even though I tried to placate Jack, on occasion I would assert myself, only to wind up worse off than before. At times, the abuse would be totally unprovoked, like being told I "looked like a whore" when I thought I was appropriately dressed.

This kind of damage was continually being added to an already guilt-ridden person. I kept thinking, "If only I could be good enough, or quiet enough, or be perfect, everything would be alright."

My instincts told me that there was something terribly wrong with my husband and our marriage. But hadn't I said those words on God's altar, "till death us do part?"

First Marriage

My role as the hero in an alcoholic family, and as a peacekeeper, made me into a faulted human being who was killing herself trying to be perfect. This impossible task kept me in an almost unbearable situation year after year. I felt that there was no way the situation could change.

Twice I walked away from my marriage. I left the first time after only six weeks of marriage when Jack struck me in the face, only to return the next day when my mother-in-law called, crying and pleading with me because her son had a gun and was threatening to kill himself.

The second time was after seven years of marriage. Our first child was a little more than a year old when I returned to my parents' house, certain that I could never go back, ever again. The break was serious enough to send my husband to a psychiatrist for the first time.

Counseling with Roman Catholic priests only reinforced my guilt. "Go back and obey your husband" was the advice I was given. This was issued by a young priest who smoked incessantly, never taking his eyes off of my legs during the entire session, somehow seeming to get a sick, vicarious thrill from my sad situation. My non-Catholic husband also sought the help of a priest, threatening to stay at the rectory until his wife returned to him.

After six months, I was confused by all the messages I was receiving. Jack said he would get help by starting treatment with a therapist and that he would change for the sake of the marriage and child. From my mother, I heard, "Go back for the sake of the child; she needs a father." Back I went, sick at heart, because, by this time, I had no love left for this man, only fear of what his anger might do.

Naturally, I was back less than a day when the old behavior returned once more. He refused to go for help after the devout promise to do so. It was only more of the same. My sense of despair continued to grow while I was trying to lead a normal life for the sake of my children.

With two daughters, a part-time career, and all the millions of duties of being a mother and wife of a well-known artist, my life went on, devoid of any thought on my part of my personal growth and happiness. There was no Ginger. I truly did not exist. The only art that mattered was my husband's. My art, because it was of a commercial nature, had no value — at least in my mind. Everything was subordinate to my husband, even the art talent that God had given me. Each added insult and indignity I suffered was pressed inward with all of those that came from my childhood, pushed in so deeply as to be almost totally repressed.

For instance, at the edge of my psyche I knew some terrible trauma had been done to me when I was three or four years old. All I could remember as an adult was that I had been in a dark place and I had been terrified. Many years later, after my awakening to the fact that I was a real true person, I developed the courage to work with a counselor to fathom the dark place. With the help of Gestalt therapy, I was able to recall being put in a dark shed or closet by teenage boys who lived next door to my grandmother's house where I had been born and lived the first five years of my life. I was able to go through the entire grieving process and forgive my tormentors. At the end of the session, I finally broke down and sobbed for a long time like a three-year-old. My counselor and I both believe that, besides the terror of being closed up in a dark place, I was probably the victim of some sort of sexual abuse.

This first courageous act of self-discovery led to later therapy sessions in which, like the proverbial onion peeling off layer by layer, I discovered other instances of early childhood abuse that had also been repressed. I recalled that as a child of nine or ten, I suffered several bouts of fondling by an older male cousin that left me feeling bad about myself because they felt good when I knew that what he was doing was wrong. Typically, it seemed as if I was the one at fault when, in fact, I was the victim.

One further instance of repressed childhood abuse led to even more guilt. An elderly bachelor in my neighborhood used to abuse children by giving them piggyback rides while he fondled them. I was too frightened to tell anyone, again thinking that I was the one at fault. I was "bad"; it was wrong to feel good.

Chapter 6
Learning to Speak: Fear and the Fish-Pond Booth

It has been said that the number one fear of American people is public speaking. In fact, *The Book of Lists* once stated that speaking in front of an audience of five hundred is one of the greatest fears of all. Fear of bugs is number two, getting into a plane is number three, and death is number eight. In other words, people would rather die than speak in front of a large audience.

For many years, I led the way in fear of public speaking. Being a shy child, I could recall as an adult the terror that came over me when the teacher called on me to speak or to go up to the blackboard. I was so shy that it was an effort for me even to do something ordinary like pulling the stop cord on the bus so I could get off—I felt that all the people were looking at me and not liking what they saw.

So the fact that I am an accomplished public speaker, speaking yearly in front of many diverse audiences, is a true miracle. The turning point was my daring to take the risk to become a women's advocate by getting out of my comfort zone, determined to walk through the fear.

One of my favorite stories about my fear of public speaking concerned my PTA work at Wilshire Elementary School in San Antonio. I was always generous in volunteering my time to the school activities of my daughters, never failing to provide cookies and cakes for their school events. On one occasion, I volunteered to be the fish-pond booth chairman for the school's fall carnival. At the following PTA meeting, I had to stand up to give my fish-pond booth report. The frog of terror that clutched my throat made words almost impossible. My knees were shaking so hard that it was difficult to stand straight. Traumatized beyond belief, I gave my report in a wavering voice that I was sure no one could understand. Feeling devastated by this experience, I felt that I would never again be able to speak in front of an audience.

As I became more involved in professional and civic activities, I realized I would have to get over this fear. I slowly started speaking out, almost *willing* the fear in my throat to subside. And I discovered something wonderful: The more I spoke out, the more confident I became. I was pleased to find that I did have some "ham" in me! In fact, public speaking gradually became a joyful experience for me. I have been told many times that I am a most natural, enthusiastic, and motivating public speaker.

Today I spend a great deal of my time speaking to both male and female audiences throughout the country on my work as an advocate for women and children. (To my way of thinking, you can't be an advocate for women without including children because we are the birth-givers.) None of the work that I am doing today would have been possible if I had not conquered my fear of public speaking. Whenever I encounter women who say that they would rather die than speak in front of an audience, I tell them my fish-pond story to encourage them to walk through the fear, as I did.

All women who have a desire in their hearts to do advocacy work for women and children must realize that they have to speak out. This is the only way to make their voices and views heard. The fear of public speaking can even be turned into an exhilarating and pleasant experience for them. Our voices have a right to be heard!

Part Three

*The Single Years:
Counting to Ten Backwards*

Chapter 7
My New Baby

There's nothing like being a single mom to make one a risk-taker of the first dimension!

My first experience in this new world was to find out in 1963 that I was pregnant with my third daughter three months after my husband and I had separated. What a jolt, especially after sixteen years of marriage, with one ten-year-old daughter and another soon to be six.

I had been under a doctor's care for some time. In fact, I was being treated for a pre-ulcerous condition brought on by all the stress of being in an impossible marital situation. That spring it seemed that I continually felt bad, morning, noon, and night. I had a horrible taste in my mouth. I imagined the taste was like the smell of something that had been caught between the walls and had died. Whether I was full or hungry, the taste was always there. With the medicine or without it, the taste was still there. I never threw up, but I always felt that I was going to, all of the time. In my other pregnancies, I had never experienced morning sickness.

Finally, in early June, my sister, Joanie, came over to announce, "I know what's wrong with you—you're pregnant!" I told her she was crazy. I couldn't be pregnant. She said, "You'd better get yourself to Dr. Santa Cruz." Sure enough, I was almost three months pregnant. In fact, I felt life shortly after the visit to my doctor. "How could this be?" I thought.

Then I remembered that in one of my last counseling sessions with my minister he had advised me to try to live with my husband as his wife one more time in hopes that he would finally consent to see a psychiatrist and, thus, try to save the marriage. But there was no way I could conceive! When that big event took place, I was well-protected. (You know, after all these years, it has suddenly dawned on me that, perhaps, Jack had poked holes in my diaphragm. I knew that he did not want a divorce.)

I went to my minister and said, "I'm pregnant and it's your fault." Thank God that even then I was able to see the humor in this situation!

Whatever, I did conceive my third daughter, Martha, on that one occasion after many months of celibacy. I couldn't be pregnant, but I was. It was the old joke — some wise men were bound to appear bearing gifts.

The real gift turned out to be a precious baby girl who made her appearance three weeks early (as my other two had), right before Christmas of 1964. What a special gift Martha was! She made us more of a family, especially since Jack was no longer around. There is nothing like a new baby to bring joy, excitement, and round-the-clock business into a household. Melissa, my first-grader, excitedly told her teacher, "We have a new baby at our house, but no Daddy!"

Years later, I heard of some neighborhood gossip that took me to task for having this child. One woman supposedly said, "Why in the world did she choose to have that child since the husband was gone? Why didn't she abort it?" Can you imagine? How cruel some people can be. It never entered my mind to do that.

My wonderful Christian mother, when told of this unexpected pregnancy, simply said, "Ginger, you can't understand why this is happening at this time, but God is sending this baby for a reason." She was right. Martha turned out to be the greatest gift I have ever received in my life.

The pregnancy was a real trial. This time I was sick for nearly the entire nine months. Somehow, I kept a home and freelance art business going, all the while starting the long drawn-out legal process of divorce. I had to go to court for separate maintenance when I was rather far along in my pregnancy. I was so naive about anything to do with the legal system that the thought of going to court just terrified me.

Looking back, I know that this baby was meant to be. When I was about three or four months along, I had to have a plumber fix a leak in the kitchen. He called me to come hold something for him and as I rounded the kitchen door, unbeknown to me there was water on the floor. My feet flew out from under me, and I landed on my back and bottom with a thud.

As I lay there with this horrified plumber looking down at me, I said, "Oh, my God, I'm pregnant." The poor man's face went white. He lifted me up and carried me to my bed. We called the doctor and the advice was to lie still for the rest of the day. The baby stayed put.

One afternoon late in my pregnancy, I was driving my car pool and was behind a car as we both were turning off a busy highway. For some reason, the woman driving the car in front of me suddenly came to a dead stop. (Personally I think she'd had too much sherry at her afternoon bridge game!) As I slammed on my brakes, my car crashed into hers, and my stomach hit the steering wheel with great force. Of course, by this time, I was so big that I barely fit behind it!

Once again, it seemed as if fate was stepping in to end the new addition to our lives. As before, however, nothing happened. Falls, wrecks, the great emotional stress of an ending marriage — nothing was going to keep this baby from joining our family.

With my first two daughters arriving after almost identical pregnancies and deliveries, and this one being so completely different, I just knew it was a boy. My mother's third child after two daughters was my brother, Ben. I can always remember Mama saying, "No mother knows what true love is until she knows the love of a son!" To say that he was a most spoiled baby is an understatement. To this day, a great family joke is "give it to Benny because he's the only baby brother you've got." Because of all this, plus the fact that this baby was literally kicking the devil out of me, I believed that I would give birth to a son.

Nothing was as before. Late one night (actually early in the morning) when I was trying to finish a last piece of artwork before turning over my freelance work to an artist friend, I became aware that something was wrong — a rather vague feeling that something was just not quite right with me. I finished the artwork. (I'll never forget what it was — a pair of black moire evening shoes.) Trying to do artwork this late in a pregnancy was not easy, believe me. My arms didn't seem long enough to reach across the drawing table! By this time, it was about 3 a.m.

I took a shower and went to bed, but I couldn't go to sleep. It suddenly dawned on me that I was having contractions, and I didn't know how long they had been going on. I remembered my doctor saying that I didn't have to be in pain to be in labor.

Early the next morning, I called my sister to tell her of my unusual night. My due date was still over four weeks away. She and my mother came flying over, trying to hurry me to the hospital. Mom was going to stay with Mary and Melissa. Just as she was trying to shoo us out the door, Joanie remembered that we had no photo of this pregnancy, so she snapped a picture of me standing in front of the newly repainted crib. I was wearing the black maternity dress that had become my uniform.

Photos do bring out the truth, and this one spoke volumes! Here was a woman in her late thirties, great with child, and the agony and exhaustion of her situation was evident in her haggard face. The dark circles under her eyes looked painted on. Clearly, she was in the last stages of complete physical and emotional exhaustion.

On the way to the hospital, we stopped to deliver my last piece of artwork. By the time I was checked in and put to bed, the stark truth was known. As I told my doctor, "You know, if this hospital were burning down, I could not get out of this bed." He told me that all those months of emotional distress, with the worry and overwork, had brought me to the point of a complete physical breakdown. The bottom line was that I was too tired to have the baby!

I had never heard of that, but he was right. I probably hold the record for the longest residence on the labor ward of the Nix Hospital in San Antonio—five days. They had to get me rested enough to give birth.

The night before I was to be induced for the birth (even though I had been having contractions throughout my hospital stay, I still had to be induced) I called my best friend, Camille Becker, to tell her I was going to have my baby at ten o'clock the next morning. Her reply was, "The hell you say."

Sure enough, Martha Joan made her appearance at 10:48 A.M. Saturday morning, December 5, 1964. Strangely enough, she had been conceived in an act of love, and now she was here to love her mother back to health.

I started back to work again at home when Martha was three weeks old. I named her after my maternal grandmother (whom I never knew) and my only sister. I knew that she would have the strong constitution of two remarkably able women.

By this time, my zest for living and love of seeing the bright side of life had returned. I had come out on the other side of this disastrous marital situation. I could even poke gentle fun at the whole event, as the original birth announcement showed:

> Martha Joan is here
> A most precious dear
> And she's mighty proud of her mater
> Who did it alone with nary a groan
> And just microscopic help from her pater.

We have to be able to see the good in all that happens to

us. Good, good deeds did come from those sixteen years of marriage. I have three beautiful and talented daughters, and we all share a great love for each other. I also have a spirit that refuses to give in to negativity.

When Martha was just three years old, I was given the opportunity for a steadier income. One of my artist friends called me to say that a new department store was coming to San Antonio and that they would be establishing a complete advertising department. I was encouraged to apply for a job as a fashion artist. I only wanted to work part-time since Martha was still so young, and I was hired to work three days a week, which suited my plans perfectly. It was fun to be in on the start of a new venture.

Dillard's, while new to San Antonio, had been in Austin for several years and was on course to become one of the largest retail chains in the country. I thoroughly enjoyed the work and the fellowship of being with some of my long-time artist friends.

I had been on the job barely six months when the advertising manager suddenly resigned and I was approached to take his job since management knew that I had this type of experience. It was a difficult decision to make, taking on much more responsibility and longer hours which would affect my life as a single mom with a young child. As always, the financial consideration won out, and once again I became a full-time member of the workforce.

The nine years at Dillard's, from 1968 to 1976, was truly like the old saying — I *did* "have a tiger by the tail!" I had never worked so much in my life. I had always prided myself on being able to accomplish anything I started, but this job was something else. Perhaps it is telling that after I resigned in 1976, the man who replaced me resigned after just four days. I think it's even more telling that within a year or so two or three people were doing the work that I had done for nine years. I've never been able to determine whether I was smart or dumb.

I do know this: When you are a single mother rearing

children by yourself, it is difficult to be independent. My heart goes out to the thousands of women who are single mothers caught in overly demanding jobs with no opportunity to find work that would give them time with their children. My hope is that new, creative ways of time-sharing, working at home, and flex-time will give these mothers more hours to be with their children. Surely corporate America must address this problem soon if we want the species to continue!

Even though those nine years at Dillard's were some of the most difficult of my life, I can look back and be grateful for what they taught me. I had to learn how to keep hundreds of separate ads in my mind. I had to be able to talk on several phones at one time while a line of people stood at my desk to ask me questions. In an advertising office there are always deadlines. One had to be a commanding general, a mother confessor, and a stand-up comic to keep the train on the track.

Since I had been trained as a graphic artist, it was difficult not to be unfair when the artists were fighting with the copywriters. I sometimes think that I could have worked eight days a week, twenty-five hours a day and never been completely on top of the job.

Luckily, my prince on a white horse came along in 1975 to carry me away from this untenable work situation. Of course, I remember Kate Lloyd Rand, then editor of *Working Woman* magazine, saying "Prince Charming is not coming, but if he does, he's going to be on a Honda and will be expecting help with the payments." This is life as we know it today!

Chapter 8
Firing My Monster God

When I was twelve years old, an event happened that was to have a tremendous effect on my life. Apparently, my mother's conscience got the best of her, so she decided it was time for my sister and brother and me to be confirmed in the Roman Catholic church.

My mother, who had been reared as a Catholic, had married my father in Laredo, Texas, in a ceremony performed by a judge. My father's family had been Methodist and Episcopalian. I don't ever remember Daddy going to church except for weddings and funerals, but he was one of the most Christian Christians I've ever known.

At the time of my exposure to catechism, I was just getting ready to go into puberty. My sister was ten and my brother was eight. Because we'd always gone to public schools, our catechism classes were held after school and on Saturdays. Quite often we walked to church on Sundays with our mother. Many times, the three of us children went by ourselves. It was a huge cathedral-type church with many statues that always fascinated me. But it was sometimes frightening, too. I've always remembered the music and, to this day, when I smell incense I close my eyes and I'm back once again in the church of my childhood.

Sister Henry, a tiny, black-habited nun, was our catechism

teacher. I have a picture in my mind of her as a little black bird swooping around. I'm sure she was a fair and loving person, but I was such a painfully shy, vulnerable little girl that her every pronouncement struck terror in my heart.

Because I was at an impressionable age, with all kinds of strange things happening to my body and my mind, I internalized everything with such a strong sense of black and white that it would take me years of counseling and therapy to see the gray. Dear Sister Henry, God rest her soul, laid such a guilt trip on me that I spent at least thirty-five years of my life trying to undo the damage to my psyche and soul.

In those days, the Catholic church had strict rules about eating and drinking before receiving communion. The time frame was that nothing could be taken by mouth after midnight if one was to receive communion the next morning. I can remember brushing my teeth and inadvertently swallowing a drop of water. A feeling of terror came over me because I knew for sure that I had displeased God by ruining my communion the next morning. And if I forgot that it was Friday and ate meat, I just knew that I was going to roast in hell. I can look back now and laugh at these childhood memories, but they had an impact on my conscience that caused me a lot of grief.

When the day came that my siblings and I were to be confirmed, I remember anticipating what it must feel like to have the laying on of the hands. We were confirmed by the Bishop of Panama. What he was doing in San Antonio I'll never know, but it must have been quite an occasion. He was a short, stocky man with beautiful vestments, the tall bishop's miter on his head, and he wore gloves. As his gloved hands rested on my head, I was expecting some kind of miraculous happening, but all I could feel were the gloved hands. I must confess I was disappointed, though I would never have uttered a word of my feelings to anyone.

Going to church on Sundays was a regular part of our life. Even though I had scary feelings about some aspects of it — e.g., the confessional booth — I had some wonderful feelings about the beautiful music I heard. I also remember how frightened I was the first time I went to confession. I can remember kneeling in the dark, breaking out in sweat but having a hard time remembering if I had done anything bad. I can't remember exactly what I confessed to, but I recall being glad to get out of that tiny cubicle and relieved at the prayers I was given to say for penance.

During my college years, I did go to church from time to time, and I visited other churches with some of my friends. But there was an overriding feeling that dominated my religious matters that if I strayed, God would surely "zap" me. It didn't help that my mother had been reared in a small town that practiced strict religious traditions. We did not play the radio in our house after a death in the family. When my sister and brother and I were acting silly, we were often told that if we laughed too much we would soon be crying.

I'm sure that what our mother imprinted in our minds was what she had been told by her mother. Add Sister Henry to this scenario and you had one guilt-stricken, pure-hearted little girl who had a God who was truly a monster.

When I chose to marry soon after graduation from college, it never crossed my mind that I had to be married in a Catholic church. When Jack and I started premarital counseling, the priest was horrified to know that my betrothed had been reared by a Christian-Science mother, and therefore he had never been baptized or confirmed. So there had to be many dispensations before the ceremony could take place. Because of Jack's heathen state, we could not be married in the church proper. It was in a back room with no music or flowers. It was like, "Quick, while the pope's not looking!" In retrospect, I can see that a marriage that started out like that was doomed.

Years later, when my first daughter was three years old, a neighbor talked me into sending her to the church school at the small Episcopal church near my house. As I attended chapel services with her, I felt a great sense of peace and belonging. I knew that I had to fire the monster God who had made my life so miserable. I loved the liturgy and the music in the Episcopal church, which were similar to what I had known in my youth.

A beautiful transformation took place in my life as I went through the process to become an Episcopalian in 1961. I learned that there was a loving God, not a punishing God — one who wanted only good for His/Her people.

I'm sure that I owe a debt of gratitude to my former religious training because it did instill in me a strong sense of right and wrong (perhaps an overdeveloped sense of responsibilities!). However, I have come to know the joy of living each day with the assurance that I have a Higher Power who is always there for me.

> He who binds to himself a joy
> Does the winged life destroy;
> But he who kisses the joy as it flies
> Lives in eternity's sun rise.
> — from *Eternity,* by William Blake

Chapter 9
This Pedestal Business

In the early 1970s, I received a phone call from a close friend who had gone back to school at age thirty-eight to become a lawyer. She and I went to the same church and were both rearing daughters by ourselves. She had seen in the paper that the Texas Women's Political Caucus was having their state convention in San Antonio and she wanted to go. We signed up and went to the meeting, political neophytes, not knowing exactly what to expect.

As we walked into the hall, I saw a huge banner that covered one end of the room. The artwork was graphic, depicting two little women holding onto each other as they stood on a pedestal that was down in the bottom of a deep hole. They were looking up at the rim of the hole where you could see the tips of a pair of cowboy boots. The cartoon-like words coming from one woman's mouth said, "I don't know about you, but I've had just about all of this pedestal stuff I can stand." I marked that as the concrete beginning of having my consciousness raised in the women's movement.

Reared in a fairly traditional family, I had bought the notion of a woman being put on a pedestal as something loving and sacred. I had internalized all the old teachings that it was okay for boys to sow their wild oats but girls should remain virginal. Seeing that banner and listening to all the women at the meeting made me realize that I had to know what it meant to be a "free" woman.

One of the speakers was Sonya Johnson, a woman who had gained national attention because she had been excommunicated from her church for supporting the Equal Rights Amendment. As I sat listening to her story, it dawned on me how naive I was about my own history. I left the meeting with the goal to find out everything I could about the women's movement and where I fit into the picture.

I went to the library to start reading about women, and I bought a book entitled *Feminism: The Essential Historical Writings*. I was amazed at all of the brave women and men who had been speaking out about the unfair treatment of women for generations. I was thrilled to learn of women like Sojourner Truth, a Black woman who dared to speak out against slavery and for women. I learned the names of all of our foremothers in the women's movement and what they had contributed in their lifetimes. I loved the idea of that wild rebel Emma Goldman, speaking up, even back in the nineteenth century, with her famous cry, "We no longer have to keep our mouths closed and our wombs opened."

One of the real thrills of my life was in 1984 when I visited Seneca Falls, New York, where the women's convention for equal rights was held in 1848. My friend Celia Morris had just published her book *Fanny Wright: Rebel in America*. Senator and Mrs. J. Patrick Moynihan had a book-signing party for her at that famous site, and I had the thrill of walking through Elizabeth Cady Stanton's house—an unbelievably moving experience to be walking in the footsteps of one of the greatest women's rights supporters in America.

So, little by little, I armed myself with the knowledge of my own history. Though I had never been a militant feminist, to use the words of Margaret Adams, a long-time editor at *Good Housekeeping* magazine, I was an "ardent feminist"—one of those women who said, "I am a feminist, but . . . ." Now the study of my own history made me realize the terrible con job that had been done on my sisters and me, and I was determined to spend the rest of my life seeing that this wrong was made right.

I discovered that those who created the term "women's libber" used it in a pejorative sense to put women down. The word "feminism" has a beautiful, clear, truthful ring to it. Several years ago, when Marlo Thomas was speaking to a large group of women in San Antonio, I stood up to ask her to give the definition of "feminism" of her husband, Phil Donahue. I knew the answer beforehand, but I wanted the women in the audience to hear it. Phil's definition is, "A feminist is any human being who believes in equality for all human beings." I was further inspired when that wonderful Canadian author Margaret Atwood said, in a 1993 speech at Trinity University in San Antonio, that "any woman who can read and write is a feminist, whether she knows it or not."

Back to this virginity thing. What a shock it was to learn that a woman's virginity was not a "blessed mother" kind of thing but a simple matter of dollars and cents. What rage I felt when it became clear that the historical reason men wanted their wives to be virgins was so they could tell whose children were whose, for it was the eldest son who would inherit the property. It was a matter of money and greed and was self-serving. It had nothing to do with the well-being of the woman's true sense of self. How cheated I felt as a woman. Yes, we've had a true con job worked on us.

After the concept of networking entered my life, it became even clearer how important it is for women to become politically involved. Early in my first marriage, I had been on the fringe of politics, working in several campaigns, so there had always been an interest there. I had allowed motherhood to reduce my activities in politics for a while; now I realize that needn't have happened. Plenty of women take their children with them while they are stuffing envelopes. I should have been involved all along!

I had been a member of the Women's Political Caucus of Bexar County since 1973, six or seven years before networking shook my consciousness. At one time in my life, I had believed the story of the smoke-filled back room and that politics was a male domain. After I became more involved, I wanted to blow the smoke away, lock up the back room, and bring politics out into the open where women could take their rightful place. It is still a difficult task to try to talk to women about politics. I can actually see the veil come down over their eyes while I am talking to them.

The Caucus, like Women in Communications, Inc. (WICI), became a great source of knowledge and enjoyment for me. Whenever I went out the door to an evening meeting, Bob, my second husband, would jovially say, "Going out with the women terrorists tonight?" In fact, he called my work as a women's advocate "Ginger and her women's terrorist activities." No matter what we were called, we were politically active women on the right track. For, when all else is swept away, it is the only way that meaningful change can be brought about in our country. Such events as the Clarence Thomas–Anita Hill hearings are working to lift the veil from women's eyes.

Some of the most fun times and most hilarious happenings I've experienced in my adult life have been at Caucus conventions. For example, once I went with my regular roommate and close friend—a sociology professor at a local university, wife of a corporate chairman of the board, and the mother of a grown son and daughter—to a lesbian dance! We were seated at a table talking to other delegates when a handsome young person in an impeccable tuxedo asked my roommate to dance. After the song ended, my friend was escorted back to the table with a polite, "Thanks for the dance." She turned to me and said, "My, that young man was a good dancer." I had to tell her that young man was a woman. Nobody asked me to dance!

Thank God I realized after my early encounter with the Texas Women's Political Caucus that the only way any wrongs against women could ever be corrected would be through the political process. Just as with the study of the history of women, I made it my business to get my political smarts together.

I have been active in the National Women's Political Caucus for many years. When women are placed on a pedestal, they are isolated from real life. The Caucus works to see that women are part of the mainstream of American life. It is a non-partisan organization that is growing in strength and numbers. It is working to push the pedestal from the scene. If you don't belong, for your own sake, sign up now!

My hope is that more women come to the realization that they are "Middle Women" and that their voice has a right to be heard. I predict that the ranks of the Caucus will eventually become the largest organization for women in the country. This kind of power will finally bring about the needed changes in women's lives. And do you know what? We are on our way!

Part Four

Coming Out in the Open:
Creating the Philosophy of the Middle Woman

Chapter 10
Second Marriage: The Good, the Bad, and the Unbelievable

The ten years I spent as a single mother were never dull. Having a baby while your marriage of sixteen years is breaking up does not bode well for a life of leisure and serenity.

The ten years began with my spending two and a half years in divorce courts after the birth of my third daughter. The divorce was appealed, so I had to go through the entire appellate process. Horror of horrors, I lost! This meant that I was still married. It also meant that I had to pay the court costs of both parties. Yes, I had to obtain two divorces from one man, so it was understandable why I was gun-shy about remarrying.

Freedom! How wonderful it is to be free! Spending sixteen years in an abusive marriage and ten years as a single mother rearing three little girls by myself, I was ready to take off and fly. However, deep down inside, I felt that there was something missing in my life.

Of course, I was so shy of getting involved again that the minute a man looked my way I took off in the opposite direction. In fact, because of my previous experience, I had a real fear of men. I was being honest when I told my friends the single life was fine for me. My entire life was devoted to my children. One of my friends said, "Ginger will never remarry unless someone has a car wreck in front of her house and she goes out to give him first aid."

A counselor once said to me that when anyone sits on a hot stove as long as I did it feels so great to get off that it was no wonder I was hesitant about being around the opposite sex. I tried to be blasé about this with my friends, saying, "I'd rather have a maid than a man." Since I was trying to work and be mother to three daughters, this saying was certainly true, but there was still something missing....

Being the single head of a family was not a lonesome life. Luckily, I had wonderful friends, including couple-friends who never made me feel as if I was the odd person out. There was not enough time during the day or night to do everything I had to do, much less all I wanted to do.

I had a live-in maid. Yes, I was a Zoe Baird! Just about every woman with children in my part of the country who had to work to feed them was in a similar situation. We had to use the help from Mexico because the American maids would not live-in. With three children, one of them a tiny baby, having dependable help on site provided the kind of support I desperately needed, even though I worked in a studio in my home.

One Sunday early in 1974, after the morning church service, I was in the Hospitality Hall at St. David's Church in San Antonio. We were gathering for coffee and fellowship when one of the new parishioners came up to introduce himself. Bob Purdy had recently been divorced after twenty-two years of marriage and was the father of two daughters, a ten-year-old and a five-year-old. I tried to be friendly to this poor soul who seemed to be going through a trying time in his life. Since I had gone through a divorce, I knew how traumatic the experience could be. Never would I have pictured this strange, extremely nervous, but evidently brilliant, scientist as my next husband. He seemed to be pretty much out in left field.

What was unusual about this first meeting was that the Friday night before, I had arrived at an introspective moment in my life. I guess I was just plain lonesome for male companionship. I remember saying my nightly prayers and asking God if I was to spend the rest of my life by myself. I was sure that even though one daughter had already left the nest and it would be some time before the other two were out on their own, there would come a time when I would be by myself. The thought of growing old without a partner weighed heavily on my mind.

Some time later, it occurred to me that I met my future husband the Sunday after I had said that prayer. I used to tell Bob, laughingly, that he was my gift from God, but I asked him why, if he was a gift from God, could I, at times, become so angry at him?

My first marriage had been a traditional one. I had never had any problem with the idea of my husband as the head of our family. In fact, I was so well socialized that it never occurred to me that marriage was a partnership. This new man in my life said words I had never heard before, like, "We're in this together." He talked about equal responsibilities and opportunities. He said that husband and wife shared the obligations of a marriage equally. This was all new but sounded great to me. We were married within the year.

Early in this second marriage, I joked to Bob that my life had deteriorated. While I had been single, my finances had been stretched past the limit, and many times I had to write a check for food, hoping that the child-support check, small as it was, would come the next day. However, I did have a maid who waited on me hand and foot. She was absolutely marvelous, was a wonderful cook and a great housekeeper, and, above all, the most caring child-care worker any woman could want. (Poor Magdalena. If she had been able to speak English, she could have made a great deal of money at a better paying job. She was that good.) I had played bridge on a regular basis with the "Friday Frolic-Hers," played golf when possible, and, all together, had lived a rather elegant lifestyle. It was a true enigma. Often I did not know how I was going to meet my expenses for the month, yet somehow I always managed to do so. My children and I had never lived so well.

My church had been my foundation, my rock, during those single years. In those days, I felt as many women did about divorce—I was truly devastated by what was happening to me. I was one of the few people in my family to divorce. My father's baby sister, whom everyone said I strongly resembled, was my idol. She was a true Auntie Mame character who had been a flapper during the Roaring Twenties. A baby photograph shows she was one of the most beautiful babies I have ever seen. A true free spirit, if there ever was one, Aunt Helen had divorced her first husband after a short married life. Although divorce was almost unheard of then, Aunt Helen was not afraid to "go out of the box," to use a nineties expression. Having a strong, willful nature, she did what she wanted to do. The baby of the family, she was probably a spoiled brat.

Coming into the Episcopal church, as an adult and at a time when the "faith alive" movement was going strong, I was delighted to experience the close, caring, family-type support I received. It was a blessed relief to know that my children were attending a church school that was so nurturing. All three of my own daughters are successful young professionals with great people skills and abundant creative talents. I sincerely believe that they are so endowed because of the support they received early in life. It was comforting to know that I had a whole church family to help me rear my girls. In the summer, the girls went to a church camp where they were carefully monitored by caring individuals (though Mary told me years later that she had her first taste of beer as a teenager at a church camp session!).

I also had one of my first leadership experiences through my church. It helped my self-esteem when in 1987, I was elected to the vestry, the lay governing body of my church, but I was still too shy to protest when at our first meeting the minister, along with the seventeen other white males, looked at me to say, "Of course, Ginger, you will take the minutes and serve as our secretary." I meekly acquiesced.

Years later, after I had learned what it meant to be

assertive, I would have acted differently. I would have answered politely but firmly, "I know all of you gentlemen know how to write. I suggest one of you volunteer to be the secretary."

I also learned leadership skills by teaching Sunday School for a long time — fifteen straight years, to be exact. The wonderful minister who counseled me before, during, and after my first divorce believed that giving help was a great way to ask for help in return. So there I was, one fall, so sick from my first-ever bout of morning sickness that I could hardly hold my head up, teaching a class of three- and four-year-olds.

There is an old saying that the best way to learn is to teach. For me, that was certainly so. Each year I progressed to an older group, gradually working my way and my patience up to the high schoolers. My all-time favorite age group was the fifth graders, nine- and ten-year-olds. That is a most wonderful, gut-level honest age, before puberty starts its wild journey. They are so sincere, so willing to learn. One little fellow once said to me, "You know, I bet you could pack this class if you served a little cup of Kool-Aid."

Another time, when I was trying to explain the Biblical lesson of the Living Water, I told the class that there was the water we all knew but there was another kind of water. This was the water, a special water that our Lord was talking about. I said they could think of it as if it bubbled and fizzed, like soda pop. This kind of water had a life of its own and could do amazing feats. The next Sunday, a precious little girl solemnly told me that some day her mommy wanted to come to talk to me about that funny water. There were also plenty of other lessons to be learned about communication skills, on both sides!

For many years, Bob and I taught Sunday School together. Later we served as youth group leaders as our girls became older. It seemed significant that we not only had met at church but that we had both been church school teachers, both taught fifth graders, and each for ten straight years. Now we combined forces to teach together.

It was wonderful to be able to share a church life with my

mate, something I had never experienced in my first marriage. In fact, though I had been a regular churchgoer, I had been married first to a man who *never* attended church. There were times, in fact, when I thought he was the devil incarnate. I would have my daughters all dressed and ready to walk out the door to Sunday service when he would suddenly say, "Come on, let's go to the ice house for candy." Guess what those little girls chose?

One of the unlikely coincidences concerning the two husbands in my life was the fact that both had mothers who were Christian Scientists. Another was that they had both played the drums, though one was an artist and the other a scientist. Jack had played in a small band in high school, and Bob in the Yale Band. These men were so different, yet so much the same. What does this say about the woman who chose them?

It has been said that we never learn from what is easy in life but only from those difficult, gut-wrenching experiences. Believe me, I've had plenty of the latter. From the vantage point of maturity and experience (I call them my "prime-time" years), I am grateful for all of the really difficult times I've gone through. Not only did I survive, but I became a stronger person because of them. I know they have made me a better advocate for women.

Chapter 11
Hooked On Helping through Pro Bono Public Relations

Back in the 1970s, when I received a phone call from Lupe Anguiano to come to a meeting planning a fund-raiser for her organization, I never dreamed I'd become "hooked on helping"—helping women, to be exact. Lupe, who had spent fifteen years as a nun, was now starting a project in San Antonio called the Employment Network to train disadvantaged women for non-traditional jobs. She would go into the barrios to find candidates, give them an intense training period, and help them obtain jobs like heavy-equipment operators. Most of them had been single mothers on welfare all their adult lives.

The fund-raiser was to be a "5-K run." Among the four or five volunteers at the planning meeting was a podiatrist, as well as a representative from the Rotary Club whose organization would donate the prizes. Since the event would take place shortly before Thanksgiving, it was not difficult to guess what the prizes were. That's right, turkeys.

What Lupe really needed was some public relations to publicize the event. With my background in advertising and public relations, she had me pegged for the job. Naturally, it was a pro bono (free) job. As a PR professional, I had always done my share of community freebies, as we called them.

I was happy to do anything that would help women leave welfare and obtain good jobs.

I did the usual tasks, press releases and public service announcements (PSAs), but I wanted something more. I wanted a mention on the local 10 P.M. television news. The leading newscast in town featured Dan Cook, still today the dean of sports announcers in our area. Dan was my target. He had a rather cantankerous, almost dour, delivery, and to my way of thinking, was not too open about mentioning women's sporting events. But his pronouncements carried weight and he was the one I wanted to deliver the message.

I came up with the slogan, "How can turkeys help women soar like eagles?" I even drew an eagle and a turkey down the side of the press release. Since I'm the kind who does really way-out thinking, I wanted a couple of turkeys loose in the studio and on screen while Dan made the announcement. That idea didn't fly, but miracle of miracles, old Dan gave a really good plug for the race. It was a coup for me, and the race was a success.

Because of my involvement with Lupe's organization, I was invited to the next graduation ceremony. It was at that event that my role as a women's advocate was cast. I was so moved when the women told of their lives with the frustrations of no education, no profession, and no money. Their obvious pride and happiness at this new opportunity to improve their lives was a joy to behold.

One woman who had gone through the program and was now employed as a bulldozer operator told what it felt like to have a regular paycheck... how proud she was to be able to take her children to town on Saturday, buy what they needed, and even have enough money to treat them to a movie and popcorn. She was tiny, not even five feet tall, and there she was operating huge machinery. She reported that her young son put his arms around her waist, looked up at her, and said, "Mama, when I grow up, I want to be just like you." That did it for me! I've never forgotten that moment.

What I saw was hopelessness turned into hope. I saw the

dignity of their personhood restored in these women. Self-respect and self-esteem replaced a sense of worthlessness. I knew my mission was helping more women out of the shadows into the sunlight.

Looking back, I see that my life has been a preparation to bring me to this awareness. I really believe that all people of this planet have about five lifetimes of work to do while they are here, just to right the wrongs that plague humanity. Unfortunately, too few people ever begin the road to self-discovery that enables them to find their true mission in life. I'm not talking about our usual roles of wife, husband, mother, or father, but one that is uniquely ours, one in which we will have made life better for others after we leave this place.

So I became hooked on helping. Those turkeys certainly helped *me* to take off and soar like an eagle, and it has been a thrilling flight!

Chapter 12
"Ginny, I Love You"

My friend said, "Meet me in the parking lot of K-Mart at 10:45 A.M. Monday." In church that Sunday she had offered to take me to my first Al-Anon meeting. I was the perfect candidate for this group since various addictions, including alcoholism, had plagued my family for generations.

I didn't know what to expect, but I did know I was truly apprehensive and scared and was thankful to have a friend by my side. I knew little or nothing about this program and was only vaguely familiar with its partner, Alcoholics Anonymous, except that AA was for the victims and Al-Anon for those who suffered beside them. Little did I know then how important those "Twelve Steps to Recovery" would become in my life.

Most people go to Sunday church to have their spiritual batteries charged. I found that my Al-Anon program kept me "up and running" throughout the week. To me, the basic tenet of the program is the firm spiritual foundation upon which people can base their lives. I know, even after years of retreats and spiritual seminars, that it was this program that started me on the road to wholeness — known as the road to self-discovery.

Of course, it hasn't been easy. I had lived a great part of my life in that almost universal state called denial. My minister once told me that thousands, probably millions, of people live their lives on the surface, never daring to find out who they are and what they really want in this life. It does take courage to start the trip to self-awareness.

I love the "peeling of the onion" philosophy in the program. The process goes one layer at a time, and with each peeling, that precious inner child comes a little closer to freedom. It is important to remember that self-discovery is a process, a continual one, and that the goal is not perfection but peace and serenity.

Many of us have lived such crisis-filled lives that often we don't even recognize serenity when we achieve it — often we think it's boredom. It takes some time getting used to it. I know this for certain: I would not have been successful as a women's advocate without the bedrock course in humanness that Al-Anon teaches.

I often say that I have a black belt in Al-Anon. While I don't know everything about this life-saving, life-giving program, I do know that continued daily living by its philosophy lets one live life to the fullest. Yes, it's *living* that counts, not just existing.

In the early 1990s, one of my counselors suggested a unique way of keeping in touch with the precious child of God who lives in me and in all human beings. She suggested that I find a doll that looked like I did as a young girl.

It happened to be the Christmas season when I started my doll search. I went to several department stores, carefully checking all dolls, looking for the right one. The minute my eyes rested on the black-haired, green-eyed, innocent-looking baby doll, I knew I had found myself; it had pigtails and bangs, just as I had had in my childhood. As I picked up the doll to take her to the counter, the saleswoman gaily asked, "Are you buying this doll for your granddaughter?"

I replied, somewhat sheepishly, "No, I'm buying it for myself."

I had started off with a stately name like Virginia Nan White but had weighed in at a hefty ten pounds and my family felt that I did not fit my name. I looked more like a Ginger, instead of a Virginia Nan, so the nickname stayed with me. Although I liked the name Virginia, I used to make a joke by saying, "You can call me Virginia, you can call me Ginger, you can call me Gin or Ginny, but you can't call me Virgie!" So I knew exactly what I should name my doll—Ginny.

By having an overt symbol for the precious young girl who was still inside of me, I was able to use the doll to help in my self-discovery. Ginny has a special place near my bed where she is what I see first every morning and what I see last every night. I tell Ginny that I love her and that the two of us together can do anything. When I feel frightened or insecure, I can take Ginny in my arms to assure her that everything will be alright.

With the help of Ginny and all of the other tools that I have used to take care of myself, I have discovered the great secret of life: One cannot love others until one learns to love oneself. The more I do to take care of myself, the more I have to offer others. The more I offer others, the fuller and more exciting my life becomes.

Chapter 13
Who... Me?... A Leader?

During the ten years I spent as a single woman, from 1964 to 1975, my church was an important part of the lives of my children and me. One night in 1965, at a covered-dish supper, a pleasant-looking woman, Suzanne Turner, leaned across the table, introduced herself, and said, "Aren't you in the communications field?" We sat together at the supper and shared a little of our personal situations. She was a single mother rearing a young son by herself and was employed by a local television station as their national promotional manager.

Suzie and I discovered much we had in common besides our work in communications. She told me she belonged to the San Antonio chapter of Women in Communications, Inc. and that she wished I would consider joining it.

That was the beginning of a wonderful friendship. The next time we met after church service, she again mentioned WICI and invited me to go to a meeting with her. I guess she asked me not once but two or three times before I accepted. Even then, Suzie was practicing effective recruitment policies because not only did she ask, but she kept on asking until she had me attending my first meeting. And still she did not give up until I sent in my membership dues.

I lost my dear friend Suzie to breast cancer in the early

1980s, this terrible disease cutting off her life way too soon at forty-seven years of age. I owe this woman a tremendous debt of gratitude for her loving persistence in encouraging me to join WICI because that was the catalyst that started me on the road from follower to leader.

Suzie and I attended meetings together and served together on committees. Through her encouragement, I became active in a small group of five or six women within the organization who, though they did not realize it, mentored me on my fledgling path to leadership.

A giant step along that path was in the late 1970s when we worked together in a fund-raising project to help underwrite the cost of a trip to Dallas for my first national WICI conference. Over a Fourth of July weekend, we sold Yankee Doodle tamales at a neighborhood party. We each had to write an essay on why we wanted to go to the national meeting in order to obtain scholarship help from WICI. We won, so we were off to the Dallas conference that would further my development as a leader.

It was an exhilarating experience for me to meet my professional communications colleagues from across the country. It was also a hilarious experience because the Dallas hotel had booked double conventions, so we wound up with five people in a room. Things were so crowded that the only way to get in and out was to walk on the beds. It was like being back at a high school slumber party. Once more we were learning how to make lemonade out of lemons and having a fantastic time doing it.

That first national convention I attended opened up a whole new world for me. I had previously volunteered to serve on various committees, always doing a good job, but I never even considered taking a chairmanship. When I returned to San Antonio, however, I became much more active in my chapter, even heading up one of the largest events of the year.

To my surprise, I did an outstanding job, using creativity that I had not been aware I had. It also surprised me when I started receiving compliments on my work. I enjoyed working with people and found that I was effective at motivating them, and it was wonderful to find out that what I was really good at was so simple to me: It was just being me.

So one truly wonderful woman, Suzie, and one outstanding organization, WICI, were responsible for turning me, a woman with no self-confidence and no sense of her own talents and abilities, into a leader who became determined to spend the rest of her life helping other women.

I have told from public platforms in the last fifteen years how important Women in Communications, Inc., has been in my life. The support and encouragement I have received from this wonderful organization have been invaluable to the work I'm doing as a women's advocate.

While I was on the National Board of WICI, a survey was taken nationwide asking, among other questions, why professional communicators had not joined the organization. The answer came back, "Because I was never asked!" It certainly had proved true in my case. Even when I *had* been asked, it had taken more than one invitation to get me to the first meeting, and the "asker" accompanied me to that first meeting to be sure I got there.

Once I became comfortable with the members of the local group I was ready to go to work, and what fun it was! I signed up to work on various committees and discovered how great it felt to be a part of a successful project. We did have some unusual happenings while we were involved in these projects.

For instance, one time, while we were in Dallas, we small-town San Antonio girls decided to be daring and go see the newest rage, a club with exotic male dancers. It was a first time for all of us and we sat at a ringside table taking it all in with our eyes bugged out and our mouths dropped open at the spectacle on stage. One of my close WICI friends, the mother of a young son, had a rather forlorn look on her face. When I asked her what was the matter, she said, "Every time I see that boy's bare behind, I want to say to him, 'Son, does your mother know what you are doing?'" It was quite a night!

Who... Me?... A Leader?

Going up the leadership ladder in WICI was an exciting and revealing experience for me as I developed new-found leadership skills. It was enlightening to work with communication professionals from throughout the country. Here was an opportunity to meet national celebrities and even have the courage to invite them to San Antonio to speak. Many accepted my invitations.

Being at the national level in WICI taught me many lessons. I had always thought of myself as a coward when it came to speaking about issues in front of a large number of people. However, every once in a while, the Good Lord causes a steel rod to go up my backbone, and my voice blares out. When this happens, it's almost like, "Who said that?" Then I discover, "Oh my goodness, that was me."

This is exactly what happened in New York City in 1986 when Mayor Ed Koch was supposedly giving the annual WICI National Professional Conference attendees the traditional address to welcome us to the city. We had waited patiently for his tardy arrival. Then, in his speech, it seemed to me that he ranged far beyond the expected welcome. He even told us that he would be happy to take questions, while the keynote speaker just sat there. Someone in the audience apprised him of the fact that the organization had just passed a resolution on pay equity, so her question concerned comparable worth. He gave the usual business–chamber of commerce reply, which I knew to be untrue.

As was Mayor Koch's habit, he ended the session by looking around the room and saying, "How am I doing? Okay?" I heard someone say, in a loud voice, "No." Horror of horrors, it was me! He turned a surprised face in my direction. I quickly gave him my reasons for opposing his view, while the WICI president and those at the head table looked on in amazement. See what I mean about a coward suddenly developing a steel backbone?

Afterwards, a young student came up to me to say, "I want to shake your hand. My mother is a nurse, and she has spent her career struggling against the very things the Mayor tried to tell us were true." I was deeply gratified and this reinforced my belief that somehow, no matter how frightened we are, when the occasion arises to speak out, we find the courage to do so.

After serving eight years on the national WICI board, I am still involved at the local level with this wonderfully supportive organization. I speak often on its behalf. So much of the happiness in my life and the success in my career have come from my involvement with WICI.

Chapter 14
President of WICI in San Antonio

One day in 1979, I received a phone call from Sarah Harris, head of WICI's San Antonio Professional Chapter's nominating committee, saying they wanted me to be the chapter president. A feeling of panic flooded over me. Even though I had been doing a good job for the organization, my self-esteem was still so low that I was shocked they would consider me presidential material. Next came a wave of fear, and I was conscious of thinking, "I can't do it." However, the rough years I had survived had done their job of turning me into a risk-taker. Determined to walk through fear, I said yes.

I took office in the middle of the summer of 1979 and spent time with my board planning the year's agenda. Of course, humans being what they are, there were people-problems from the last group of officers, but the excitement of having the whole new year ahead of us helped overcome any troubles that might have existed.

From years of experience in the ad and PR fields, I put my conceptual planning abilities to work. I was like a bird let out of cage and ready to fly. The first program I planned as president of the chapter was in August, and I had been told not to expect a big attendance because it was only recently that the chapter had even been meeting during the summer.

I invited Ms. Ninfa Lorenzo, the owner of Ninfa's Mexican Restaurants in Houston as well as a newly-opened one in San

Antonio, to be our speaker. I titled the event "Eat Tacos and Talk Turkey With Ninfa — Find Out How One Woman Made It in the Male-Dominated Restaurant Business." A widow at forty-seven with a large family to support, this amazing woman dared to risk becoming an entrepreneur. Hers was a terrific story of individual success. The invitations went out and we had almost one hundred people show up for the event.

All was in readiness, and then I received a last-minute phone call from Houston. Ninfa had suffered a heart attack, was hospitalized, and the trip was off. I was faced with my first real crisis in leadership.

My gut feeling told me not to call off the event but to come up with an alternative. I had Ninfa's office Fed Ex her speech to me, and then I went to one of my Mexican-American friends to ask her to stand in for Ninfa. At the event, I made the announcement of Ninfa's illness. The audience was understanding and her speech was a huge success.

There were some words in that address that I'll always remember: Ninfa said that we should not be afraid of failure and that "if we knew who we were and where we came from, we could always go back and start again." Those words have remained with me to this day. This is a message that women must understand. We cannot be afraid of failure. If we never try, we can never succeed.

In 1982, I had the great honor of being named a chapter Headliner, an award that is given annually to the person who has given the chapter outstanding service. After two terms as president of the local chapter, I went on to serve two terms as regional vice-president. Then I conducted my first national campaign for vice-president of membership and held that office for two terms.

When I realized that I had changed from being a follower to being a leader and a very good one at that, I set a goal to campaign for the national presidency of WICI in 1989. After all, it was the organization that gave me the opportunity to lead. Even though I lost the election (going against an opponent who had much more money at her disposal), I still won! I can say this because I achieved a goal I had set for myself.

Chapter 15
"Ginger Purdy and Daughters"

In 1980, I started out on another leg on my journey to self-discovery when networking came into my life. I did not realize that it would become a family affair. After thirty-something years as an ad and PR professional, I discovered that all three of my born daughters were choosing to follow in my footsteps in the field of communications.

My eldest daughter, Mary, had inherited her artistic abilities from both her artist parents, while middle daughter, Melissa, had a tremendous writing talent, and youngest daughter, Martha, chose business communications and marketing as her major in college. They all joined in to help their mother bring networking to South Texas.

As I networked among the women in the eight women's organizations that formed the nucleus of networking, I had a ready-made advertising force within my own family. I called on Mary to help in designing the brochure and logo. The slogan was "Network Power — You have it, Use It", and she designed a clever piece of artwork with a woman's hand holding a lipstick that wrote the word "Network" in bright red. The word "Power" in strong black letters had a woman's mouth for the letter "O."

We received many brickbats from the militant feminists who, in those days, were against anything that looked feminine. This was one reason why I could never join the ranks of the extremists. Though I supported the cause, it seemed silly to me to think that we had to look and act like men to be considered equal. I was a feminine woman and I was not about to make excuses for it.

Melissa (now a feature writer with the *Houston Chronicle*) and I came up with some strong copy for the brochure. We talked about network power, what it was, how to get it, and how to use it. We talked about woman power, how we've always had it but didn't know it. We discussed how we could learn to use it to our advantage, especially when we tried to move into and up in the male-dominated business world.

Martha was still in high school but she was already beginning to spread her wings as a good communicator. Even in high school, she worked for me as a marketing representative for one of my clients, thereby gaining valuable experience. She helped in planning a venture called "Ginger Purdy and Daughters," a small novelty effort that sold T-shirts and information about networking through a national ad in *Savvy* magazine. Mary designed the art, Melissa wrote the copy, and Martha helped administratively.

As late as I was in having my consciousness raised about what it meant to be a feminist, this experience with my three daughters was a valuable lesson in risk-taking. The ten years I had spent as a single woman rearing my daughters by myself had made them realize that we were in this together! As long as we were together we could do anything.

All women have within them the power that can be nurtured through the use of networking if they will just make the effort to do so. Men have used their "good old boy" network for so long and to such an extent that they are not even conscious of having one! Women, being relatively new to the marketplace, have much to learn and a lot of lost time to make up. The word "networking" may have been new in 1980, but the process was not.

Ginger Purdy and Daughters was an exercise in freedom

to try to reach as many women as possible with the message about what network power could do for them and their daughters. Through the years, when I have reached a low point, it has always been a spirit-lifter to pull out one of the Ginger Purdy and Daughters brochures to see what we accomplished. It gives me a great feeling of pride when I read those words.

I've always been grateful that I knew who I was in the women's movement when the call came to be interviewed on the television program *Good Morning America*. I'm also grateful that I had the courage to voice my philosophy when I was interviewed. That propelled me further as an advocate for women. The more I dared to speak out, the more courage I developed. As Scott Peck says in *The Road Less Traveled,* "The truth will make us free. But it will make us miserable first." That fits in with my Twelve Step program and the Al-Anon saying: "We are as sick as our secrets."

Chapter 16
Still Scared but Speaking Out: "Network Power/Texas" is Born

In the fall of 1980, I returned from attending the national WICI conference in San Diego where I had had an almost spiritual awakening about what networking could do in my life, and it was my husband who gave me the courage to put my dreams into action.

The conference that year was held at a hotel on the edge of the water in San Diego Bay. There had been a gala night out on a Mississippi-style riverboat. I had always thought it was rather comical to have that kind of boat out in California. It even seemed funny to me the next day when I read the conference agenda to learn that the Network Power seminar that I was interested in would be held on the riverboat. I guess they ran out of rooms at the conference center.

As we assembled on the boat for what was to be the most important workshop I ever attended, one woman had to leave. She couldn't stand the almost imperceptible rocking of the boat. I've often thought of that woman missing out on the opportunity that changed my life—but then who knows if it would have been the same for her?

Apparently, I was ready to hear what Alina Novak, a pioneer in networking and the treasurer of the New York City WICI chapter, had to say. The thought of putting networking and power together and the consequences it could have for women opened up a whole new world for me. I guess it was kind of a "Damascus Road" experience. Like Saint Paul, I saw the light!

As soon as the seminar was over, I started networking on the boat. I received a commitment from Alina to come to San Antonio and show us how to do this thing called networking. I was certain that if we learned the concept, we could have power as we never had before.

Back in San Antonio, the experience I had out there stayed at the forefront of my mind. I had never before experienced such an awakening that had captured my entire being. I became even more aware of networking and the power it generated.

Bob simply said, "You have to practice what you're preaching about networking." So, I picked up the phone to call women I did not know. I started "walking my talk."

First I called Kay Moore, who was working with the Women's Opportunity Workshops at San Antonio College, and asked her to meet me for lunch to talk about my plans to bring the concept of networking to San Antonio. She called me back within a few minutes to ask if she could bring Jean Collins and Cessie Sanchez with her. They enthusiastically accepted my idea to have a networking seminar in 1981, with proceeds to go to WICI's national ERA fund. They had no problem with that since it was going to help women.

Next I called Mary Jesse Roque of the newly-formed Mexican-American Business and Professional Women's Club, and found her eager for her group to come on board. I was beginning to learn how to network and was having a great time at it!

Latrell Johnson, then president of the National Association of Negro Business and Professional Women, was the third to join us. Then came Rosemary Stauber of the Bexar County

Women's Center, Carole Bufler of the American Association of University Women, Helen Butler of Women in Business, and Roseanna Szliak of the YWCA.

This was the core group of eight women's organizations that came together to bring the first Network Power seminar to San Antonio. I was putting into practice what my mentor Alina Novak had encouraged us to do in San Diego: I was the leader, the start-up person, the mover and shaker. There always must be such a person to take the bull by the horns.

How could someone who was just beginning to spread her wings be so sure of what she was about? Where did I get this moxie? I guess it came from "all of the above." By this, I mean everything that had happened to me in my life. All of the so-called "hard times" were the teachings times to help me get ready for this, the most important work of my life.

It's interesting to look back and recall the feelings I experienced several weeks before the big event. We already knew it was a sellout and that this networking seminar was going to have far-reaching effects for San Antonio women. I remember telling Bob that the thought of standing up in front of five hundred professional women was giving me cold feet.

For the first time, I realized that I did not know who I was in the women's movement. During the sixties, I had been aware of such a movement, but my life had been totally absorbed with my job as a single mother. All I knew was that I was turned off by the extremists at either end of the women's movement.

When I told Bob of my fears, it was then that he asked me to perform that experiment that changed my life, and I said to myself, "Yes, my voice has just as much right to be heard as anyone else's." Now I knew it was okay to be that Middle Woman. My husband gave me permission to be myself. How wonderful to know that it is okay to be yourself, that you don't have to change anything about yourself to become involved in a movement!

After our coalition of eight women's organizations produced that first successful seminar, we realized that we had started something too good — too important for women — to let go. We had started something in San Antonio that was going to change women's lives for the better. We spent many hours talking about what kind of organization we should form to continue what was obviously a much-needed support group for women.

During discussion of creating a new women's organization, we spent time talking about the word "power." We wanted the organization to be called "Network Power/Texas," and we knew that most women were afraid of the word "power," thinking — wrongly — that it was in the male domain. But we were sure that the time was right for us to go for all the power we could achieve, for it was necessary to have it in order to do what we knew we must to help women. The purpose of Network Power/Texas was to promote equity and self-sufficiency for women through educational programs, activities, and services.

After Bob helped me define who I was, my life took on a new energy and direction. At one point, he said to me, "I didn't think you'd get quite this active." My answer was, "It's too late, buddy; you've already opened the door." Of course, he had to hurrah my blossoming speaking abilities by telling our children, "Can you believe she's getting paid for talking?" Then I would get back at him by saying, "Okay, see if I give you any of this honorarium!" What a glorious sense of freedom people feel when they finally discover that it's okay to be who they really are and that they can have great success just being themselves. Many times since that day in 1981, I've had cause to be grateful to my husband for opening my eyes to this fact.

In my lectures, I spell out clearly the definition of a "Middle Woman." I've always said that the term "working woman" is a redundancy. I've never known a woman who didn't work either in or out of the home. The real tragedy in our society is that housework has no value. This terrible injustice must be corrected someday soon!

Since 1981, I've gone all over the country giving a seminar entitled "Networking and the Middle Woman: A Positive New

Outlook." I've included my personal story of how I came to discover, without apology, who I was in the women's movement. Before, I had always been ashamed to tell women exactly what my position was, fearing that if I could not identify with the extremists in the movement my position somehow wasn't valid. Without my husband's help, I would still be saying, "I'm a feminist, but..."

The truth of the matter is that unless you can be who you are at the deepest level, you cannot throw yourself wholeheartedly into any cause. When I had the courage to say that I was a "Middle Woman," something interesting started to happen. No matter in which part of the country I was speaking, at the conclusion of my presentation, there were always women coming up to me saying the same words, "Ginger, until I heard you speak, I never knew who I was in the women's movement. I am one of your Middle Women."

I would answer, "Of course you are; three fourths of the women in our country are like you and me. When we speak out with one voice and show up at the voting booth en masse, we will start to see miracles happen."

Now guess who has trouble with my Middle Woman philosophy? It certainly isn't the secure men — the ones who have a good sense of their own personhood when it comes to issues between men and women. Those colleagues accept the fact that women should have the same rights as men. They also know that it is only right that pay equity become the law of our land. The real culprits are those men who are unsure of themselves. They are the ones who, despite all the trappings of macho-ism, have dark, secret fears about their own worth as human beings. Consequently, they have to have someone to look down on, to treat as second-class citizens. These are the men we need to give a wide berth. I almost consider them a lost cause but would like to think they could be rehabilitated, and perhaps some can.

My concern about women who are "Honorary Males" is expressed in a statement in Carolyn Warner's book, *The Last Word: A Treasury of Women's Quotes,* where she quotes my definition:

> Unfortunately, there are still many women in the business world who refuse to support women. I call them "Honorary Males" — women who think that power is to be had only in the company of men. Women must realize that they have power — economic and political. Don't give your power away; use it for yourself and for the benefit of other women.

However, my most fervent hope is that the mothers who are rearing sons today will see that their boys receive the necessary nurturing to make them "the New Men" (the wonderful term used by Margaret Adams), who will be women's equal partners in the coming years.

One of my delights as a Middle Woman and as an ardent feminist is seeing this hope come to pass in the way my first grandson is being reared. My daughter Melissa and her husband, Mark, are raising Sam to be a feminist, a "New Man." When her son was just a toddler, she was reading nursery rhymes to him one day. When she read Jack and Jill and came to the part where "Jack fell down and broke his crown and Jill came tumbling after," Sam's immediate question was, "What did Jill break?" If this doesn't show that he is being brought up to think of women as equals, I don't know what it is!

Part Five

Going National with the Middle Woman Philosophy

Chapter 17
"Good Morning America"

It was either clean hair for *Good Morning America* or chicken salad for Women in Communications. Which would win out?

One day in June 1981 during my second term as president of the San Antonio WICI chapter, I received a phone call from the daughter of a friend who was working for ABC television in Atlanta. The young reporter knew that I was the mother of five daughters. *Good Morning America* was doing a segment on the status of the ERA one year before the end of the extended deadline for ratification. The reporter also knew that my life and work as a woman's advocate and as an ardent supporter of the ERA would be a good source for an interview. She told me to expect a call from the ABC office in Dallas to set it up.

The next morning I was busily planning a WICI meeting. The members of the old and new boards of my WICI chapter were to meet to exchange information in preparation for the coming year. Traditionally, this meeting was a potluck supper, and I, as hostess, was planning to make chicken salad for the entree.

At the same time, I had volunteered my chapter to take press credentials for the Secret Service in preparation for President Reagan's imminent visit to San Antonio. Both events were planned for the same day, one in the morning and one in the evening.

The call from ABC came around 10:00 A.M. Charles Murphy, the interviewer, announced that he, his cameraman, and his soundman were flying to San Antonio at noon for the interview. This unexpectedly short notice threw me into a panic.

On top of this, those WICI colleagues who had agreed to help me take press credentials dropped out at the last minute. How could I carry out all those commitments: make chicken salad, take credentials at a downtown hotel, and wash my hair? Did I dare go on *Good Morning America* with dirty hair?

Yes, I did make the right decision. The chicken salad won out. After I made the salad, I went down to the hotel to spend the rest of the morning taking press credentials on the phone. I had told the crew from ABC where I would be, and they caused a minor panic when they marched into the secured rooms of the Secret Service with camera running and lights glaring. The head of the Secret Service advance team came rushing out shouting, "You can't bring TV in here. This is a secured area." Imagine his surprise when he was informed that they were looking for Ginger Purdy.

The ABC team followed me about for the rest of the day, filming my various activities. They also asked permission to set up their equipment in my home to film that night's WICI board meeting. By that time, word had gotten out that *Good Morning America* was in town interviewing me, so every member of the board, old and new, showed up. Jean Dawson, one of the WICI board members, had not been notified of this special happening. As she walked into the glare of the lights, she had enough presence of mind to smile and whisper through her teeth, "What in the hell is going on here?"

Before the women arrived, the camera showed me serving a plate of food to my husband in the living room. What I was actually doing was trying to speed him on his way to a school board meeting so that I could have the house to myself for the meeting.

All in all, the crew filmed several hours for a segment that appeared the following week on national TV for a grand total of a couple of minutes; however, that time was enough for my friends and communication colleagues all over the country to catch the interview. I received their excited phone calls for days afterwards. That was the first time that my "Middle Woman" philosophy was viewed nationally.

Charles Murphy, the interviewer, was so impressed that he tapped me on the knee to say, "Lady, write that book. Your story needs to be told." So, in 1981, I determined that some day I would tell my story of the woman in the middle of the women's movement.

Chapter 18
Creativity Takes Off: Founding Two Organizations

As time went on, my life became more hectic as I responded to more and more requests for speaking engagements all over the country. The idea of a book stayed in the back of my mind. Several times, I shared with my communications colleagues my desire to write a book. Some threw cold water on the subject. They said, "You've waited too long. The concept of networking is now old hat." However, in my heart, I knew that a power greater than myself would show me when the time was right for the book.

Once on the road to self-discovery, amazing events can occur! I know they occurred to me; but the idea that I would found four organizations between 1981 and 1991 would have been totally impossible to comprehend. However, after my awakening to what the concept of networking could do for me, and after I made a commitment to make it work in my life, I discovered talents I never suspected.

In the words of my poet friend Wanda Diekow, "I never knew I was in a cage until I was let out." She was talking about her sense of freedom after getting out of a long, unhappy marriage. I knew exactly how she felt. It is truly one of the most exhilarating experiences one can imagine.

During this time, I founded two of the four organizations

I would establish in that decade. The first was a support group called "Friends of WICI," and it came into being because I had trouble saying "no."

In the early eighties, I had been successful with my tenure as a WICI president. We had become one of the most visible women's organizations in town, and our membership was at an all-time high and growing. Because there were specific requirements to join the organization (one had to be working in some creative area of the communications field and have at least two years of experience), many women who wanted to become members were not eligible. Many wanted to network with our organization in order one day to be able to get jobs in the communications field. It bothered me to have to turn them down.

One day, while flipping through our church directory, I came across a section at the back of the book called Friends of St. David's. This middle-sized Episcopal church that I had attended for many years was the only church in the town of Terrell Hills, right in the middle of San Antonio. Because it was near a large military base with a teaching facility, we had many families that attended for short periods while one of the spouses was taking courses. Some of them returned to San Antonio many times in the course of their military careers and then often they would retire here, so they attended the church for varying lengths of time, not actually being members but "Friends."

A light bulb went off in my head. Why couldn't I do the same for the women who wanted to join WICI? I received permission from my board, called our national headquarters to make sure that what I wanted to do was permissible, and publicized the fact that we would have a support group called "Friends of WICI."

Our first meeting was a beautiful garden reception at San Antonio's fabulous new Museum of Modern Art. We had a wonderful turnout and over twenty-five women signed up as Friends. Through the years, this group has been a tremendous asset to the organization. For a modest annual fee they receive our newsletter and attend all our events. The organization is the real winner because the Friends help in innumerable ways, such as sending out invitations and serving as hostesscs for events.

One of the most gratifying aspects, to me, about the Friends of WICI is that one year, through the association, five Friends became eligible to join WICI as national members through networking efforts that found them jobs in the communications field. The word soon spread throughout the national WICI organization, and several more chapters instituted this support group. This was the first concrete evidence I had of my organizational ability. It seems like once I dared to take that first step to become a leader, I started experiencing those hidden talents. Thank God I took the risk!

After our coalition of eight women's organizations had produced several successful seminars, some of the original members were no longer the presidents of their organizations. We were also at the point where we were not sure how to proceed. Carole Bufler, the former president of AAUW, suggested that we needed to formalize into a nonprofit organization. Since I had been the originator of the coalition, I called a meeting to set this idea in motion, and "Network Power/Texas" was born.

It was evident we had created a much-needed element in our city because of the tremendous interest women showed in learning what networking could do in their lives. We called in the services of Bonnie Ornelas Symonds, who had recently passed the bar exam, to help us obtain our status as a nonprofit corporation. Thirteen of us donated money for the next step. Even though the original group had been together since the fall of 1980, we were officially chartered by the State of Texas in 1982.

The unique ability of this organization to meet the needs of women was its unlimited scope. Its monthly meeting, City-

Wide Network Night, was a two-hour session held on the fourth Tuesday of each month at a local restaurant. A notice was always placed in the newspaper, but word of mouth was the most popular and successful way of getting the word out. The event did not take up a whole evening. In fact, it was designed to give women a short period on their way home from work to network for whatever goals they might have.

We've taken careful notice of who attends these meetings. It has never failed to amaze us, year after year, that three-fourths of the women in attendance each month are there for the first time. This has let us know what a tremendous need we are meeting. Attendance fluctuates each month. We have had as few as twenty and as many as two hundred. The numbers really don't matter. We know that those who are there are the ones who were meant to be there.

Network Power/Texas is administered by a volunteer board of nine women, in addition to the president. The board has purposely been kept small to maintain a close feeling among the members, and several have been on the board since its inception. At the monthly board meetings, the board sits at a round table in close proximity to each other. It is a loosely conducted session with laughter and camaraderie.

What is unusual about the group is that it has never been involved in the tedious nit-picking prevalent in many women's organizations. Attesting to this is the fact that the bylaws have been amended only once in fourteen years. The board keeps its mission at the forefront — women helping women to succeed.

In order to be fair to all those attending City-Wide Network Night, it is structured so that everyone has a chance to participate. The hostess for the night is a board member who takes a turn once a year as hostess, and it is her prerogative to choose the speaker and the subject for the meeting. First order of business is a five-minute period to meet as many people as possible and exchange business cards. The woman receiving the most business cards wins a free order of cards from former board member Wanda Rohm, owner of

Presto Business Cards in San Antonio. She has generously donated this gift for many years.

Periodically, the program is varied by a sharing night. Attendees are asked to share with the group whatever was their greatest obstacle or greatest help in their life's work. These are special evenings because women are inspired and instructed by listening to the stories of others. The most fulfilling times for me are when I hear women tell about coming to City-Wide Network Night, how they found an opportunity there and pursued it, and how it changed their life for the better. This is an affirmation that everything we are doing has tremendous value for women in our area.

We realized early on that one of the ways we could help women through our networking efforts was to make them realize the importance of their educational development. Too many women leave school early and eventually wind up as single parents trying to rear children with minimum-wage jobs and food stamps. We have found in years of networking that these women are eager to obtain the training they need to give themselves and their children a better quality of life.

One of the ways the Board found to bring this about was to create a curriculum called "Networking for Success," a flexible program divided into six segments about leadership training. We knew that women had to be the leaders in their own lives before they could go on to be leaders of others. This meant they had to recapture their lost sense of self-worth.

A friend had sent me an article about the results of a national survey identifying leadership traits important for women's success. We based our program on these traits: self-confidence; assertiveness; integrity; persistence and determination; empathy, or a concern for others; and a sense of humor. We have found that by using this curriculum, we are able to help women blossom in their personal and professional lives. It works!

Another educational project was the establishment of the Network Power/Texas Scholarship Fund, which gives four educational scholarships each year, three to the colleges of the local community college district, and one a rotating scholarship among the other colleges and universities in town. The proceeds from the events sponsored by the organization go into the Scholarship Fund. At every meeting, my youngest daughter's graduation cap from high school is used as a receptacle to gather scholarship funds. We hope, someday, to have our scholarship fund built up to such an extent that we can help many more women.

It is gratifying to me that something as simple as picking up a telephone to call someone whom you do not know to network with about a dream can have such amazing results. There have been many other organizations in my city that had their start as a spin-off of our original networking group. This, too, has been satisfying for all of us who believed in the concept of networking and decided to make it a part of our lives.

In the almost fifteen years since my trip to San Diego in 1980, the work that we have been able to do through the concept of networking has affected literally thousands of women's lives. We have seen countless women who were caught in the cycle of abuse find themselves through our programs, open the door of their cages, and soar into the unlimited sky of freedom. I really believe that the women who were involved in the startup of Network Power/Texas were guided by a Higher Power.

Chapter 19
"Can Networking Do Anything for a Woman Like Me?"

Several years after I embarked on the networking road, I was giving a seminar on the subject to a group at the Women's Opportunity Workshops at San Antonio College. By then, I had become good at public speaking. It was a relief to know that I could just be myself, telling my story, and that it had a real impact on my listeners. I was beginning to feel that I had a real gift for motivating women to change their lives.

After I said "goodbye" to the group, I started down the hall but stopped when I realized someone was following close behind me. I turned around and saw a woman with her eyes downcast. In a shy, hesitant voice, she said, "Mrs. Purdy, can networking do anything for a woman like me?"

Her name was Dolores B. and she had been attending the women's program. I told her that networking could do anything for her that she wanted. All she had to do was dare to take the risk to start changing her life. I started meeting with Dolores, and, as we became better acquainted, she shared her story with me. This was my first mentoring effort as a woman's advocate.

I found out that Dolores had a difficult life. After leaving an abusive family situation, she dropped out of high school and married at an early age. When we met, she had spent twenty-eight years in an abusive marriage and had six children. Now she had discovered that her husband, who had abused her sexually, had also been sexually abusing their daughters.

She had received her GED and was determined to finish her education. I encouraged Dolores to keep on with her studies and to start working on her self-esteem. At that first meeting she was so unsure of herself that she could not even look me in the eye. I could feel her deep unhappiness and her desperate attempt to reach out to me. Since I had spent many years in an abusive situation, I had a kinship with this woman. I made up my mind I was going to see she had the opportunity that she deserved.

In our talks together, Dolores confided that she desperately wanted to keep up with her schoolwork but that she had to have some kind of job to bring in money for her family. Network Power/Texas was in the process of establishing criteria for scholarship funds. I put Dolores' name forward as a qualified recipient because of her dire financial situation. I was delighted at our next Network Power/Texas conference to introduce her as our first grant recipient. We awarded her $500 to purchase an electric typewriter so she could do clerical work in her home, thereby allowing her to go to school during the day. I was so moved by the look on her face when she received her award that we *both* cried we were so happy.

Dolores became a close friend of mine, and I continued to encourage her to improve herself. As her sense of self-esteem grew, she was realizing she did not have to put up with unacceptable behavior, so she ended her marriage. She still lived in a housing project, she still had problems with her children, but she kept on with the process of changing her life. I was beginning to see some wonderful changes taking place in the woman who had seemed so downtrodden and hopeless when I had met her.

Some time after I had started mentoring Dolores, one of our City Council members, Maria Antoinetta Berriozabal, was planning an event called "Hispanas Unidas" or Hispanic Women

United. She was interested in having the subject of networking for one of the workshops. I had already become known as "the mother of networking" in the city, so it was natural for the two of us to get together about doing the workshop.

Over lunch, we discussed how we should present this subject since many of the women had never attended a seminar before, and the idea of women getting together to talk about networking was totally new to them. We decided to call it "Chicano networking," and I told her that I had the perfect person to join us in this effort. Naturally, I was talking about Dolores, who I knew would be a fabulous role model for these women. They could relate to everything she had to tell them.

It is important to picture what Dolores looked like when I first met her. How we view ourselves is closely tied in with our estimate of self-worth. She had on slacks and a shapeless overblouse. Her hair was pulled back in a straight ponytail and she wore no makeup. She had a look about her that said, "It really doesn't matter what I look like. I'm a nobody."

The day of the seminar, I was so proud of Dolores! This was a completely different person from the one I had met the year before. Here was a good-looking woman with a short, attractive new haircut, and wearing a trim navy-blue suit. She carried a briefcase and looked every inch the professional woman she had become. It was an amazing transformation.

Both the City Council member and I were used to speaking in front of audiences, but this was Dolores' first experience as a public speaker. We had talked about the fear of speaking in public. I encouraged her by saying that we were in a safe place and that many of the women were probably in the same place in which she had been when we first met. I also told her to be herself and to tell them her story. I witnessed the beautiful flowering of a new woman who was then ready to mentor others. Here was another example of my favorite mantra, "If I can do it, anyone can."

Through the years, Dolores and I have kept in touch — at least by phone when we couldn't get together. Her life hasn't been easy, but then neither has mine. We have a special bond that is precious to both of us, a bond that will never be broken.

I sit on the Advisory Board for the local "I Have A Dream Foundation", the wonderful organization that Eugene Lange started years ago to help underprivileged children stay in school by assuring them a college education. I recently attended the annual fund-raiser, a casino night held at a local country club. I had heard that Dolores had gone to work for the Foundation as a project coordinator at a local elementary school. It had been several years since we had seen each other.

Dolores and the rest of the staff were dressed in elegant tuxedos. She looked wonderful. I walked up behind her and said, "Hello, Dolores." She whirled around, shouted my name, and grabbed me in a bear hug. We stood there so happy to see each other that we were soon crying tears of joy.

I have such pride in Dolores and love for her and am filled with such a sense of gratitude for what I have seen this woman do for herself. She is now mentoring a group of disadvantaged minority elementary school students to stay in school. From all reports, she is doing an absolutely outstanding job.

Dolores had the courage to reach out to me for help. I had the desire to share with her whatever experience and knowledge I had. Together, we were able to work wonders in both of our lives. In mentoring, it's a win-win situation.

Chapter 20
The Late Bloomer: From Follower to Leader

It has been said that to accomplish something great, we must not only act but dream, not only plan but also believe. I believe in women, in their immense capacity for sharing and caring. I also believe in what women can accomplish when they help each other.

The most important part of attaining what you want is knowing *what* you want. I want everything for women that any other human being has! By the time I knew who I was, what I wanted, and how I was going to get where I wanted to go, everything about me had started to sag except my spirit, and the spirit is what counts!

Yes, without any sense of embarrassment, I call myself a late bloomer. My premise is "Thank God I bloomed!" I was well into adult years before I had enough sense of my own personhood, enough self-confidence, to stop listening to other people's plans for my life. For too many years, I had tried to be everything that everyone else wanted me to be, instead of that person my Higher Power had intended me to be. I had been on the road to "superwoman" for many years without knowing it, trying to be the perfect daughter, the perfect wife, and the perfect mother. As I gained that invaluable sense of self-worth, I realized that trying to be the "perfect anything" is truly the road to insanity.

Coming into the awareness that I did not have to strive to be perfect was like opening the doors of a cage and flying. It was one of the most freeing moments in my life. Then, through networking with women from all over the country, my sense of freedom increased tenfold as I listened to their stories.

An outstanding example was in 1982 when I heard Mary Lou Dobbs, insurance woman extraordinaire and author of *The Cinderella Salesman,* give a presentation on her life story. Starting out as a single mother with a limited education, no saleable skills or talents, and an eighteen-month-old son to support, she had parlayed her sense of determination in order to succeed in a truly spectacular career.

She taught me that in order to succeed we must risk. We must walk through fear. I did not have to be afraid of failure, which is only a delay, not a defeat. I also learned from Mary Lou's great sense of humor to laugh and not worry about the minor concerns. When she said that she had discovered that "dust keeps," I was freed from another one of my perfection hang-ups — that one's house always had to be spotless.

I am grateful to all the women who have been willing to share their stories, both the positive and the negative. Through this sharing, we have helped each other reach our full potential as human beings under the trying circumstances that tend to hold women back even today.

One of the reasons I am so appreciative of networking is that it teaches women to reach out to each other, to serve as resources, and to set goals for themselves. Through the centuries, "those in power" have used women through means subtle and not so subtle to work against each other. Unless we talk together, we cannot learn to trust each other. It's not a question of who is going to throw the first stone. It's a question of who is going to build with it.

For too long, women have allowed minor differences to cause major divisions among them. I know the time is *now* for women to build together for a better life for themselves, their children, and their families.

The Late Bloomer: From Follower to Leader

This late bloomer has learned an important fact: A leader has two important characteristics. First, she is going somewhere, and second, she is able to persuade others to go with her. I am on a crusade to unite America's "Middle Women" through the use of Network Power. I hope that every woman who reads these words, whether or not she is a late bloomer, will be persuaded to join me in my crusade. "Middle Women unite!"

Chapter 21
The Ego Trip: Suffering the Slings of Others to Stand Up for Yourself

Is anyone born with thick skin? In the summer of 1984, I took advantage of my husband's upcoming business trip to Europe to set up a trip of my own through what I had learned about networking. I thought, "This international seminar will look good on my resume."

I contacted a friend living in Germany, a long-time WICI colleague, who was in the process of organizing a women's center for one of the military bases in a German city. I told her Bob was going to be in Paris consulting with a client and that we planned a European vacation in conjunction with his work. She was delighted to know I was coming and arranged a workshop on networking for military women and for spouses of military men.

We flew to London and as Bob departed for France, I caught the boat train to spend five days in West Germany. I had spent many years traveling by myself in the U.S. and Mexico but never in Europe. I thought, "Heck, if college kids can travel all over Europe by themselves, this old gal certainly can." It was a wise decision because I was able to spend time in Amsterdam visiting the museums and other places of interest. As an art major in college, I had fallen in love with Van Gogh's work so it was wonderful to go through his museum.

The Ego Trip

Deep down, I felt empathy with this tortured man who never seemed to be appreciated during his lifetime.

It was great to see my WICI buddy again and to have her introduce me to her friends, both those working in the military and those on the German economy. She gave a party to introduce me to her friends and even arranged a meeting with German women who were just beginning to spread their wings politically. It was an enriching experience to see how much we had in common but it was disappointing to realize that, no matter where I was in the world, women were caught in low-income jobs and middle-management positions.

While I was there, I learned that one of my communications colleagues back home had written to my hostess saying I was on "an ego trip." There was a horrible sinking feeling when I heard those words. Because of the inferiority complex I had carried from childhood, plus the strong shame core, I was devastated. Being a people-pleaser, I was deeply distressed to think a "friend" would say something like this about me. I had never had enough ego to go around the block, let alone take a trip!

Back in those days, I did not have as much networking experience as I do now. I have learned since that people filter all information through their own experiences. Consequently, there can be any number of reasons why people say what they do. I learned that suffering the slings of others was to be expected by anyone who set out to be a leader. I also learned that the "green-eyed monster" has much to do with unkind treatment toward a public person.

There was one other lesson to be learned about rude remarks and backstabbing methods that has nothing to do with the individual involved, and that is projected anger. It was amazing to me to learn that people projected anger on others that had to do with problems in their own personal life with which they could not deal. I understood then what San Antonio's Mayor-Emeritus Lila Cockrell meant when she said that those who step forward for public life can never take personally what is said about them.

So how does a people-pleaser react to such a situation? Something that helped me was going to all the seminars and workshops I could find on building self-esteem. For me, it was making a decision to start looking backward in order to go forward. I had gained enough information to know that in order to find my own self-worth, I had to look inward. I had also learned that whenever a myth surfaces, I must search for the hidden truth within it.

What I had to work through about being on an "ego trip" was that quite possibly I had said something or had acted in a way that someone construed as my suddenly being "full of myself." Looking from that perspective, I remembered that soon after I was elected to a regional office in WICI, Ann Richards, who was just starting her campaign for Texas Treasurer, had come to San Antonio for a meeting with that group. I had asked the hostess, somewhat innocently, whether or not it would be alright for me to sit at the head table, since I was now on the national board of WICI. Because of that timid request, someone concluded that I was on an "ego trip."

Today, I find it comical that the first time I dared to speak up it was taken in a way that was totally opposite to the way I really felt about myself.

Some other helps on my road to self-discovery were the great spiritual truths and slogans involved in my Al-Anon program. Concerning self-confidence, there's a wonderful slogan: "Fake it till you make it." This idea began to make sense to me, especially since I had educated myself about the perception of power. I learned that if we think we're powerful, we are. So much of the time, perception is reality.

Another great lesson in my quest for self-knowledge was the wonderful freedom to be gained from taking charge of my own life. I feel no shame when looking someone in the eye and saying I had to wait till middle-age before I could say I was in charge of my own life. I'm just thankful that I finally learned not to give my power away.

There is nothing that I know of except a Twelve-Step program that shows one how to take control of one's life. Being in charge requires voicing your power, especially on the telephone. I was truly amazed at the results. When I made a phone call with the authority of my self-esteem firmly in place, as opposed to the timid-sounding way I used to operate, I was gratified to hear, coming from the other end of the line, a kind of respect that any human being wants to be accorded. Talk about feeling good about yourself, the first few times I tried this, it was like someone had handed me a gift. In reality, it was a gift I gave myself.

In the middle sixties, I was an early Transactional Analysis enthusiast. A friend of mine — a single parent rearing three young girls by herself just like me — joined me in signing up for one of San Antonio's first TA classes. We had met teaching Sunday School at our church. Since both of us had been through traumatic divorces, we were ready to do anything we could to feel better about ourselves.

The book *I'm OK, You're OK*, by Thomas A. Harris, had just come out and we really wanted to be "okay." To show how far I've come in this business of self-knowledge, back in those days my mind was so scattered — especially when it came to talking about myself — that it was just like a ping-pong ball wildly ricocheting around a closed room. Add to that the tremendous amount of self-doubt that I carried, and it's a wonder I was able to finish the class. However, there was something deep down inside that kept saying, "If you're ever going to dig yourself out of this pit that you are in [of always being a victim], you have to hang in there and dare to change." Many positive results came from that TA class. By the way, this was at least fourteen years before I really started "peeling my onion" in Al-Anon. So the groundwork had been laid and that first timid step toward self-discovery really paid off for me because it started to bring many issues to the surface. I was okay, and it was wonderful for me to know that others could be okay too.

Coming full circle, I have found that all of the events that have seemed so horrible and debilitating in my life have been the real building blocks of the free woman I am today. When I am tempted to fall back on those old tapes, it's freeing to remind myself that no one can hurt me, unless I allow it. The more firmly I take control of my life, the more freely and lovingly I am able to give to others.

Chapter 22
Courage

One night at a City-Wide Network Night, when Network Power/Texas was several years old, a woman called me "the Mother of Networking in San Antonio." I don't remember her name, but I do remember my reaction — one of surprise and delight. I have always been a maternal woman. I love everything that has to do with mothering, especially taking care of tiny babies. I seemed to be a natural. In fact, my family often called me "Earth Mother." You can imagine my pleasure at being called the Mother of Networking in San Antonio.

Of course, like the obsessive-compulsive person I am, I had jumped into networking, so I took it as a compliment when I was called the Network Nut of San Antonio. Since networking had actually changed my life, any title like this, funny or not, was bound to meet with my approval.

At another network meeting, a woman came up to me to say that she had been finishing her education so she had not been able to come to City-Wide Network Night for several years; however, now she was back and there was something she wanted to tell me. She said that since she had known how devoted I had been to networking and helping other women, she thought of me as the "Mother Superior" of networking. I enjoyed a laugh over that. I told her I was giving her my blessing and for her to keep networking to help other women in her life. Since that time, I have often used these titles to describe myself in opening remarks at speaking engagements. For me, this takes courage!

As time went on, I received more and more invitations to speak, both in San Antonio and beyond. In fact, the more I traveled to share my story and the Middle Woman philosophy, the more supporters I gained.

I had enjoyed the opportunity to do my first international networking in West Germany. This had been a tremendously exciting opportunity to share my philosophy with American women connected with the military. It also gave me a chance to talk with German women. As I updated my resume after this trip, I could list speaking engagements on the local, state, national, and international level. "Hey," I told myself, "that's not bad for a late bloomer."

By then, I had increasing name recognition. If it had to do with networking, people just automatically assumed that Ginger Purdy was going to be involved. In fact, it was quite surprising, but satisfying, when people started coming up to me saying, "Oh, you're Ginger Purdy. I always wanted to meet you and shake your hand." The first few times it happened, I was almost embarrassed. The more it happened, the more I came to realize that when one is given important work to do, these are some of the affirming events that happen. You just accept them graciously and thankfully.

Soon my name was well known throughout the state. In fact, it was so well known that my Women's Political Caucus of Bexar County friends came to me with a request to campaign for public office. Now, I had been politically active for many years, realizing that the only way we could ever correct some of the wrongs done to women was to address them through the political process.

I've learned, at this point in my life, never to say "never." As for a political future, I live my life one day at a time. All I know is that, at the moment, I am blooming where I'm planted. I know I'm doing what I'm supposed to be doing at this point in time. The realization of what it means to be a leader, both the advantages and disadvantages, is always in the forefront of my mind. If I have learned anything in the past fifteen years from my work as a woman's advocate, it is that you must have the courage to "walk your talk." You cannot be any kind of a leader unless you have a strong sense of empathy for the people with whom you are working.

This means that integrity must be at the core of what you're doing. Over time, any kind of falseness or insecurity will surely surface unless you're sincere about what you are doing. I do know that kindness is the strongest force in the world and that if you live your life by the Golden Rule, treating others as you would like to be treated, not only will your mission have success but it will grow. Have the courage to be yourself, to be a vocal Middle Woman!

Ginger with Governor Ann Richards and Anita Heim, 1994

Ginger with Shirley Chisholm,
Trinity University, 1986

With Shirley Chisholm,
St. Philip's College, 1995

Networking with women in
Jalapa, Veracruz, Mexico, 1992

Ginger with Jane Macon and Pat Smothers,
receiving the "Women Who Make a Difference Award"
from the International Women's Forum, Denver, 1992

With the National Institute for Leadership Group, Xian, China, 1995

Ginger at International Women's Forum's Spring Retreat in Mexico City, May 1995 (opening reception)

With Liz Carpenter, Austin, Texas, 1988

Members of San Antonio Professional Chapter of WICI celebrating chapter's 42nd anniversary

10th anniversary of Network Power/Texas with representatives of the original eight women's organizations

Ginger with daughter Melissa in Huairou, China, 1995 at the United Nation's 4th World Conference on Women

Ginger with three of her most long-time friends, Peggy Peterson, June Daniels, and Camille Becker

Ginger with Mom on her 90th birthday, brother Ben and sister Joanie

Ginger and her mother, Mary in their Canary Islands costumes, 1993

With daughters Mary, Melissa, and Martha

With stepdaughters Janet and Alison

Ginger's girls, with their husbands, and children

Ginger with granddaughter Rylee Margaret Owens (singing "I love you a bushel and a peck") San Antonio, 1992

Ginger with the first two women she mentored, Dolores and Connie, San Antonio, 1992

Alpha Kappa Alpha Choir singing Julia Knight's song, "I'm Glad I'm A Woman." San Antonio, 1993

I'm Glad I'm A Woman
Words by Julia E. Knight
Music by Bernice Lucille Bland

I'm Glad I Am A Woman
I'm Glad That I Am Free
I'm Glad I Have The Courage
To Be What I Want To Be
I'm Glad I Am A Woman
And All The World Can See
I'm Glad I Am A Woman
I'm Glad, Glad, Glad For Me.

Because I Am A Woman
I'm Bound To Lead The Way
I Lead And Others Follow
Each And Every Day
I'll Keep The Country Moving
Convey My Point Of View
I'm Glad I Am A Woman
And I Can Do What I Want To Do.

I'm Glad, Glad, Glad, Glad, Glad,
Glad, Glad, Glad, Glad, Glad, For Me!

I'm Glad, Glad, Glad, Glad, Glad,
Glad, Glad, Glad, Glad, Glad, For Me!

Chapter 23
"Women's Legislative Days"

In the spring of 1984, at a conference on women's issues at Southwest Texas State University in San Marcos, a group of women were sitting in the hospitality room when the talk turned to what a mess "Women's Lobby Days" in Austin had been that year. This was an event at which women from throughout Texas went to the state capital to lobby their legislators on issues important to them.

The particular meeting they were talking about had been held in an Austin restaurant filled with women. The noise level was so high we could not hear ourselves talk, much less hear the speakers.

Someone in the hospitality room at the San Marcos conference said, "You know, we really should get Women's Lobby Days organized." A yellow legal pad was passed around, and those who wanted to be involved signed up. I don't know if it was Peggy Romberg of the Texas Family Planning Association who uttered those words, but she has been the chief organizer ever since.

What had always stood out in my mind about Women's Lobby Days was the kind of reception we received from our legislators. To say that they were less than enthusiastic about our visits was an understatement. The unspoken message was, "You gals are not a force of importance, so why should

I bother?" From my point of view, we were so insignificant that the whole time they were supposedly greeting us they were looking over our shoulders, and the hands that they held out were gently propelling us out the door—talk about feeling insignificant!

So we started planning something called "Women's Legislative Days," to convene every other year during the biennial session of the Texas legislature. It was held at the Lyndon Baines Johnson School for Public Affairs and the Joe Thompson Conference Center at the University of Texas campus. The steering committee was made up of a dozen or so representatives of women's organizations from throughout the state who would meet monthly in Austin throughout the preceding year. The agenda for the conference included those issues coming before the legislature at its next session. Workshops were held on these issues by experts. There were always nationally prominent keynoters speaking on the cutting-edge issues of the time. The state chapter of the National Women's Political Caucus had its major fund-raiser at that time, at which they roasted a well-known political celebrity.

At that first conference in 1985, almost a thousand women from all over the state gathered in Austin. It was a tremendous success. We saw something amazing happen on the second day when we went to lobby our legislators. They looked us straight in the eye, and, with great enthusiasm, led us into their offices for a nice chat.

The word had spread ... fast. They all said the same words, "We heard that you women had almost a thousand attendees at your first big conference." They were giving us eye contact alright, just like they were giving us their attention. It was the result of Shirley Chisholm's famous dictum: "Organize and strategize to achieve your goals." From that point on, we knew we were no longer insignificant when it came to politics.

Being a part of the planning process of Women's Legislative Days all these years has been significant to my development as a women's advocate. It has allowed me to network with many women from throughout the state and country. It has contributed greatly to my growth as a politically astute voter.

Each time this event takes place, more and more women are pulled into the political circle, and the ripple effects of their participation impact their communities. I hope that this book, helping free up women to be who they are without any reservations, will have an even greater impact on the political process.

We are already seeing more and more women running for political office on the local, state, and national levels. If my dream comes true, in my lifetime we will see the first woman president of the United States.

Chapter 24
Lessons From "Dear Abby": Using All of One's Communication Skills to Spread the Message

One reason Network Power/Texas was so great for women in San Antonio and surrounding areas was the yearly seminars that brought outstanding women to our city. For seven years, this organization brought women from all over the country: Jo Foxworth, author of *Boss Lady* and *Wising Up: Mistakes Women Make in Business and How to Avoid Them* and one of the first women to own an advertising agency in New York City; Liz Carpenter, Maureen Reagan, "Dear Abby" (Abigail Van Buren), and many others.

Each of these seminars took about a year for the board of Network Power/Texas to plan. Since networking was the buzzword in the early eighties, the excitement to learn about this new concept was high, so all of the seminars had great attendance. The word had spread from our first successful seminar that had over five hundred in attendance. Now hundreds of women wanted to join in the networking.

One of the ways I found national personalities for these seminars was through WICI. During nearly eight years on the national board, I attended the national conferences. Because of my commitment to make networking work in my life, I was not shy about approaching these women to come to San

Lessons From "Dear Abby"

Antonio. What I discovered in this process was that all of these women were just as approachable as my local communications colleagues. I did not have one of them act like a prima donna. It was an enriching experience for me to meet these fascinating women.

A seminar that especially stands out in my mind was the year we had "Dear Abby" come to San Antonio. Some months earlier, I had gone to Fort Worth to attend the annual Celebrity Breakfast produced for many years by their WICI chapter. They had the most famous women in the country speak at an invitation-only breakfast that got 700 to 900 women up early to attend the unique 7:30 A.M. event. Year after year, the Fort Worth WICI chapter was able to give more scholarship money from this event than any other chapter in the country. That is where I first heard Dear Abby, and I was determined to bring her to San Antonio.

For years, I had read Dear Abby's columns and those of her twin sister, Ann Landers. At times, I chuckled, and at other times I was moved to tears. Meeting this tiny "giant" of a woman was an unforgettable experience. Her visit to San Antonio was co-sponsored by the *San Antonio Express-News* which gave a lovely reception for her the night before our event. I was able to learn first hand that Dear Abby was a warm and caring person with a great sense of humor. Through her columns she was able to communicate with people all over the country. Using her writing skills and human understanding, she could impart healthy, wholesome advice. At the seminar, she read from a select group of letters she had received over the years. She had the audience absolutely roaring with laughter over some of the missives and her answers to them. It was all great fun . . . and also great inspiration to hear the letters of more serious intent.

These conferences and the chance to meet these women-leaders helped me hone my communication skills. I received great support in spreading my message of "women helping women to succeed." I was determined to dispel the myth that women could not work together. Just as I had come to understand that so-called "women's issues" were not really women's issues at all but human and economic issues, I also came to understand that the myth of women not being able to work together was just that — a myth. At times, everyone has problems working together in close contact. It is not based on gender. Since men have been out in the work force longer than women, they have more experience working together.

While I was involved in producing yearly seminars for Network Power/Texas, I was also being inspired by attending many other seminars, workshops, and lectures given by both men and women. What I tried to learn from the men was what they had to offer that was positive, like team playing, competitiveness, and assertiveness in following one's goals.

On the other hand, I wanted women to become strong enough to change some of the negative parts of the work place, like the wage gap between the salaries of women and men, the institutional discrimination that keeps women from achieving high positions in their chosen fields, and the sexual harassment that is prevalent throughout the workplace.

Just as Dear Abby has played a part in dispelling the myths that keep women down, I know that my Middle Woman philosophy can be a great freeing agent in helping all women move up!

Part Six

The Making of a Middle Woman

Chapter 25
Learning to Take Care of Myself

After the concept of networking came into my life and I made a commitment to make it *change* my life, I went farther on the road to self-discovery. It was like any journey into the unknown: There was a great deal of fear at first, not knowing what I might discover while I "peeled the onion." However, after several small successes in taking care of myself, my sense of self-worth started to grow.

Several years ago, I was walking through the Dallas-Fort Worth Airport on my way to a speaking date in another big city. I was excited at the prospect of talking before such a prestigious group and had been looking forward to the trip for some time. I had carefully researched my message and spent a great deal of time making sure the speech was perfect in every way. I was wearing a new suit I knew was becoming, so I was striding confidently down the concourse to board the plane. This was several years into my development from follower to leader, and I had been working on my self-confidence, self-esteem, and assertiveness. I looked like the speaker that I had become.

By now I had discovered that all human beings, male and

female, shared a common trait. No matter how self-confident they appeared on the outside, circumstances can arise to reveal the tentative child within them.

As I walked along, feeling upbeat about the trip, I became aware of being closely scrutinized by two casually dressed young women leaning against a wall. As I caught their eyes, I saw one poke the other in the arm and jerk her head in my direction with a smirk on her face that said, "Look at the strange hairdo on this old gal who's coming." (I have always worn my hair in an unusual style with short, straight bangs. I like bangs, and since I'm busy, I keep them short to save time and trouble. It's a matter of practicality.) I knew by their expressions that my looks did not register as "okay" with them.

Before my awakening, I would have allowed such a look to destroy my sense of self-confidence. In a flash, I knew what to do to keep my sense of serenity. This was important so I could give an effective speech and deserve the honorarium I was to receive.

Fortunately for me, both of these young women had aspects of their appearance that I knew they could not be happy about. They were both dressed in blue workshirts and blue jeans. Each was at least twenty to thirty pounds overweight. Both had protruding tummies which were magnified by their tight jeans. Catching their gaze, I looked at the girl closest to me and pointedly allowed my eyes to travel down to her stomach and then back again to her eyes. Then, I deliberately did the same with the other girl.

There could be no mistake about what my action was telling these two young women. Most people have some aspect of their appearance with which others can find fault. Without being cruel or vicious, people can, however, through appropriate action, take measures to protect their self-esteem.

As my eyes returned to their gaze, the young women had looks of remorse and they lowered their eyes apologetically as I passed. I felt a great burst of pride. I had taken an action to let them know that I was pleased with the way I looked. I had confronted their disapproval of me. Now I could board the plane with my sense of self-confidence intact.

This one small episode became a giant marker for me in the process of learning the important task of taking care of myself. I am grateful to those two overweight young women in the D/FW airport.

Spending over three-fourths of my life as a people-pleaser — someone who always felt the other person had to be right, no matter what the circumstances — it was almost impossible for me to take up for myself. Coming from a long line of co-dependent women, I often tolerated unacceptable behavior

One day, as I was driving toward the main post office in San Antonio, I made another discovery in my quest for self-confidence. I was in the right-hand lane, making a right turn into the post office parking lot. Suddenly, on my left a car came zooming around, the driver trying to cut me off. This was dangerous because it was a one-way lane. I had to slam on my brakes to avoid a collision. Apparently, this was a game of chicken with the young man who was driving the car. I assumed he was trying to race me to a parking place because he gave me a rather smart-alecky look as he cut me off and pulled into the parking place that should have been mine. I parked my car, walked into the post office, and went up to the young man who by now was standing in a long line of people.

I put my hands on my hips, looked him straight in the eye, and said, "People like you give me a pain in the ass!" I turned on my heel and went about my business, leaving him standing there with all the people looking at him. He looked like he'd been kicked in the stomach.

For him, perhaps it was a lesson to correct his reckless driving. At least, I hope it was. For me, it was another example of how I could take care of myself to avoid that old familiar sick feeling of being a victim once again. I'm happy that I have stopped being a doormat and have started taking care of myself.

Chapter 26
Shirley Chisholm: Women Speaking with One Voice—"Organize and Strategize"

For several years, I had been increasingly interested in having one of my "sheroes" come to Texas. Shirley Chisholm had long been one of my favorite feminists. This brave African-American woman had spent fourteen years in Congress going up against the "old boys' network" time after time. She had also endured the most degrading types of discrimination, because of both her race and gender. She had even campaigned for the Presidency of the United States and was treated by many people with disdain and disinterest. Since then, she has devoted her life to going around the country organizing Black women politically. Her clarion call was, "Never again will we be forgotten."

Shirley had been one of the founders of the National Organization for Women (NOW) and the National Women's Political Caucus. Like many of the early radical feminists, she had gradually come to a more middle-of-the-road position, not unlike what Betty Friedan describes in her book *The Second Stage*.

I am so thankful for Shirley Chisholm's pointing me in the right direction back in 1986 when I invited her to come to San Antonio to give a speech titled "Women Speaking with One Voice." Through Shirley, I learned that the way to obtain power was to "organize and strategize." Although women as a group did not have money, we did have numbers. Organizing over one-half of our population to be politically active was certainly a worthy step to give women the political power they needed to correct existing inequities.

The Network Power/Texas organization had been asked to provide a Friday night special event for the first meeting of the National Association of Women's Centers at a conference held in San Antonio. Rosemary Stauber, the director of the Bexar County Women's Center, and a member of the board of Network Power/Texas, had known of my interest in bringing Shirley Chisholm to town. She suggested that I contact her for this event.

I was able to reach Shirley at her home by telephone, instead of through her speaker's bureau. This was fortunate because the organizations involved did not have sufficient funds to pay a national speaker's bureau's going rate.

At that time, Shirley was teaching at Mount Holyoke in Massachusetts. After several calls — and because Shirley knew that this was a special, first-time event for a worthy group — she agreed to come to Texas. The meeting was held at Trinity University, and Shirley did not disappoint the group. She gave one of the most thrilling speeches they had ever heard. The standing ovation that she received from an audience of women of every color and station in life was the most heartfelt that I have ever witnessed.

The next day, when we had a chance for personal conversation, she voiced her concerns on the lack of involvement of women in their own circumstances. I also shared with her the fact that my "Middle Woman" philosophy had evolved in order that I might know where I stood in the women's movement.

Shirley described the historical situation of women like this: For generations, she said, women have been banging their heads against a brick wall. They would fall down, bleed awhile, then rise up to repeat the process. Time after time, she said, women would hit the brick wall in the same spot, only to fall down and bleed some more, never accomplishing anything positive, only hurting themselves each time. This had gone on year after year.

What women should do, according to Shirley, was fall back to organize and strategize about other ways to get around the wall. The obstacles will always be there, she said, so women just need to devise ways to get around them.

From my perspective as a Middle Woman, Shirley's advice made sense. I already knew that the majority of women in this country were "Middle Women," though they might not realize it. From my fringe involvement in the beyond-war movement, I knew that if even 5 percent of the population were interested and involved, a movement would grow. If 20 percent were involved, it would be unstoppable. So all I had to do was to communicate my Middle Woman message to 20 percent of the women in the U.S.

In reality, the whole purpose of my writing this book on the Middle Woman is to reach this 20 percent. I live for the day when all of the Middle Women in this country will stand up to speak with one voice. This is the day when we'll know within our hearts that we have achieved the power that is necessary to bring our issues to the forefront of society and prevail!

Chapter 27
The Network Power/Texas Seminar and the Commitment Lesson

When my girls were growing up, I was firm with them about commitment. With me, it ranked right up there with one's good name and reputation. Many times, one of them would make a date with a friend, only to have something better come along — usually a cuter boy! There was always much wailing when Mama stood firm and said, "Nothing doing. You go with your commitment." I'm sure it made them angry, but I knew that some day they would thank me for instilling this value in their character.

So what I did in 1987 when Network Power/Texas VII was canceled three weeks before its due date was no surprise. I had gone to Europe with Bob after the plans for the program had been made. The seminar was called "Feeling Good, Looking Good" and it dealt with women's health issues. Working with the local women's hospital, we had planned a large number of speakers to deal with subjects important to women.

We invited Dr. Paula Caplan from the University of Toronto who had written *The Myth of Women's Masochism*. Coming from Boston was Judy Norsigan, one of the principals with the Boston Women's Health Collective, a nonprofit women's education and health organization that produced

Our Body, Our Selves and later *The New Our Bodies, Our Selves*.

Immediately after my return home I had plans to undergo cosmetic surgery for a drooping jawline that had kept me feeling less than one hundred percent about myself. I was even to be one of the workshop speakers doing a presentation entitled "What You See Is Not What I See" with my plastic surgeon.

While I had been away, several members of the board decided, on the spur of the moment, that they were just too tied up with other concerns (family and personal problems) to finish the last-minute planning, so they convinced the rest of the board members to cancel the event! When I returned and found out what they had done, I hit the ceiling. This was a commitment. To my way of thinking and in my value system, a professional organization did not act in this manner. Countless people had already volunteered their time, and financial commitments had been made.

As president, I told the board that our reputation as an honorable organization was at stake. Since I was founder as well as president, mine was too. I was willing to take full responsibility for raising the necessary underwriting to produce the event, a task that had been delegated to the board members. I found out later that the real reason some board members wanted to cancel was because they did not want to go into the community to raise money.

By this time, I had undergone the surgery, and although I still had bruises covering my chin, I did what I had to do. Out into the community I went with no makeup on my face, a real sacrifice for a vain woman. It was a stretching experience for my ego. (I did wear a purple blouse to match my purple bruises.) In one week, I raised the necessary funds.

Each community leader I called on told me that what I was doing was right. They told me my organization would have lost its integrity after so many people had committed to help us. I have to admit it was one of the most difficult tasks I've ever had to do; but it was one of the most rewarding in terms of my personal and professional integrity. I knew at my most basic level that what I had done was right. It was a learning experience for all concerned. Even the ones who had started the canceling craze knew it had not been honorable to do so.

There are times when a leader has to do just that . . . lead. Granted it will not make everyone happy and you'll suffer many brickbats. However, it will save the reputation of your organization. Difficult decisions are just that . . . difficult. It is a point of pride with me that I have never shied away from them. After all, as a child I was taught that a commitment is a commitment.

Chapter 28
The Pay Equity Campaign

When I was elected national vice-president of membership for WICI in 1986, I spent much time thinking about the effects on membership by the failure of the valiant effort to pass the Equal Rights Amendment, which had disappointed so many members of main line women's organizations. Many of these groups were also experiencing a drop in membership. From my experience in the Women's Political Caucus, I knew the Choice issue — abortion — while critically important was too divisive ever to mobilize women. I was looking for an issue that would.

Pay equity was certainly one that hit all working women where they lived . . . in their pocketbooks. After talking to my committee members from various parts of the country, I set to work to create a campaign. I wanted my organization to be the national leader for women in the battle for equal pay. After all, I reasoned, if professional communicators could not communicate the message, who could?

I created a brochure that had a red handbag on the front. The flap on the handbag lifted up to disclose a slotted area where one could insert coins. This money equaled the current wage gap between men and women — in those days, women's pay was sixty-four cents to every dollar a man earned. I had adapted this idea from the famous March of

Dimes campaign from some years earlier.

The campaign received the approval of the National Committee on Pay Equity. Executive Director Claudia Wayne loved the idea of the red purse. She said the movement needed such a symbol.

I also contacted colleagues in the Business and Professional Women's (B&PW) group and other organizations. All were enthusiastic about my plan and expressed an interest in joining the project. I was excited and delighted to think this might put WICI in the forefront of this important and necessary change in the workplace, hoping it would produce a bandwagon effect, with professional communicators all over the country clamoring to join our organization.

The 1986 National Professional Conference of WICI was to be held that fall in New York City. "What a perfect place to start this important campaign," I thought. I knew from past experience that some kind of media event was needed to launch a campaign. I envisioned all the members of the women's organizations that worked in Manhattan receiving a letter telling them that on a certain day on their way to work they should stop by the conference hotel to throw an old, worn-out handbag in a roped off area — another telling symbol of the pay gap! (All women have old used handbags stored away in closets.)

The *pièce de résistance* of this media campaign would be to have the whole lot packed up and sent to Washington to gain the attention of President Reagan and Phyllis Schlafly! It was an off-the-wall idea, but what fun I had just thinking about the stir it would cause.

Alas! When I presented the campaign idea to the leadership in the spring before the national meeting, I received a less than enthusiastic response. In fact, I was told to cease with the idea, it was not a membership campaign, and that the whole project was "unprofessional."

This was one of the real low points of my service on the national board. Even though parts of the campaign were a little on the wild side — the old handbags — I knew the red purse as a symbol for pay equity was a winner. It was sad that my organization failed to see its value.

Of course, months later when I read in the newspaper that the Business and Professional Women had introduced a red handbag as a symbol for pay equity at their national meeting in Hawaii, I wasn't too surprised. I would be lying if I didn't admit that this was one of the truly frustrating experiences of my life. Some years later, I paid five dollars for a little red purse lapel pin sold by a local B&PW organization.

Oh well, that's life! You win some and you lose some. But I do wish people would be more open and willing to take chances. We spend our time and money going to seminars and workshops which tell us that in order to succeed we must learn to be risk-takers, but few people dare to take the leap.

Ginger Purdy's little red purse is out there doing its job. Even if no one else knows this, it gives me a certain amount of pleasure to know the origin of the idea. If, eventually, it has some value in equalizing wages for women, then the frustrations, insults, and indignities that I suffered will have been worth it.

I've always known that I'm a futurist. The plain fact is that my organization was not ready for me. Some folks see the forest, some the trees, and some even the bark on the trees. I'm soaring up there looking down on it all. The world needs all kinds. However, unless you have that far-off vision, brave new leaps are not possible. This was one instance when I wish women could have seen beyond the forest.

Chapter 29
Founding the San Antonio Women's Chamber of Commerce

When Network Power/Texas was about eight years old, the board members spent some time assessing where we had been and where we wanted to go with our organization. We created a curriculum called "Networking for Success" (see Chapter 18) that we taught at various retail establishments and institutions throughout the city. Like our original concept of networking, this course proved to be extremely successful, showing once again that women were not only open to all forms of self-improvement but eager for them.

We kept the fee modest to make it affordable for the greatest number of women. At a leading department store we presented the course for six Monday nights in the fall. We were told that our courses received the largest show of interest of any they had ever advertised, which once again proved we were offering what women needed and wanted..

About that time, I heard of an Austin group's efforts to start a Women's Chamber of Commerce of Texas. It seemed as if Network Power/Texas was at the right point to start a second organization. I had heard that if a group was trying to improve its standing in the community through organizing and strategizing, it would be to its advantage to operate more than one organization.

So I presented the idea of a Women's Chamber of Commerce to the Network Power/Texas board, and in the fall of 1987 we began dialogue with the Austin group. We spent the spring of 1988 making plans for our San Antonio Chamber, and had our first meeting June 15. We were welcomed by many community organizations in town. Through the generous support of Southwestern Bell, our opening champagne reception was a tremendous success.

The San Antonio Women's Chamber celebrated its eighth birthday in June of 1995. In that short period it has become an accepted part of community leadership in San Antonio. Its members serve on many boards and commissions, and its innovative Leadership Loop training program is open to any woman, unlike those which require nominations or other restrictions.

Once again, if I had listened to the naysayers such as those who told me in 1980 that it would be too much trouble with too few results to bring a networking seminar to San Antonio, neither Network Power/Texas nor the San Antonio Women's Chamber of Commerce would have come into being. One of the greatest lessons I learned was that when I made a commitment to make networking work in my life I had to listen to my inner voice.

I knew that I had another winner with my first organization, Friends of WICI, and I knew I had a winner with a later organization, "Ann's Fans," a support group for the future Governor of Texas, Ann Richards. Network Power/Texas and the Women's Chamber of Commerce came into being because I listened to that inner voice and was persistent in my determination to see them succeed.

The secret of success, I think, is to keep a positive attitude, a belief in yourself and your abilities, and to know that whatever you have in mind can come to pass. My favorite motto is still "If you can dream it, you can do it." I did dream it, and I did do it!

One of the reasons a Women's Chamber of Commerce is so important is the way business in corporate America and the world seems to be going. Anita Roddick, founder of the worldwide, world-famous The Body Shop company, gave a rousing speech in 1993 at a fund-raiser for Network Power/Texas in San Antonio. This amazing woman has set out to change the way business is done in the world. Her book, *Body and Soul: Profits with Principles: The Amazing Success Story of Anita Roddick and the Body Shops,* not only tells the story of The Body Shop but gives a view of how this change can come about.

In her presentation to us, she gave some amazing statistics about the time it will take to level the economic playing field for women—something like nine hundred years! That may have unconsciously been one of the frustrations that propelled me to establish a Women's Chamber of Commerce in San Antonio. It's truly gratifying to see what can happen when a group organizes to change the status quo in their community, and this is exactly what we're trying to do with our Women's Chamber. Like Anita Roddick, we know there has to be a better way of managing business and the world. To me, it seems as though women are being pushed to the forefront, almost in spite of themselves, to have a hand in making life better.

When we first started organizing our Chamber, word came to us that a prominent local lawyer had said, "A women's chamber of commerce—that's the most asinine idea I've ever heard." From his point of view, I'm sure it was. However, from ours, never being able to have a place at the table when important community decisions were made, it made very good sense. We were seeking more money and more power for women. The way to achieve both (bless you, Shirley Chisholm) was to organize and strategize.

Early in our efforts to organize the Chamber, we gained strong support from Marise McDermott's op ed article, "On the Necessity of Developing A Woman's Chamber of Commerce," that appeared in the June 7, 1988, edition of the *San Antonio Light* newspaper. Her insight seems to express, word for word, what we were trying to do. In the following years, I guess I have sent out hundreds of copies of her commentary to women and organizations all over the country. It just made so much good sense.

Of course, as with any other organization, there have been growing pains. I stayed involved in the day-to-day management as executive director for five years, and retired in 1992, receiving the title of Founder and President Emeritus. It was time to give others the responsibility of managing the organization. It can be difficult to let go, wondering if those who follow will have the same passion and desire to go forward. Knowing the foibles of human nature, I sometimes wonder how any group stays together over time. However, if the mission of the organization is on target, we will survive, in spite of ourselves!

Part Seven

Political Awareness Pays Off

Chapter 30
Founding "Ann's Fans"

In the 1990s, I finally made the leap into the political trenches, no longer merely a voter-observer but now really involved. And I had the perfect candidate to support . . . Ann Richards!

I had met Ann through the National Women's Political Caucus when she was a county commissioner in Austin. Then she decided to campaign for statewide office as Treasurer of the State of Texas in the 1982 election. Here was a candidate whom I respected because she had all of the issues that I cared about at the forefront of her agenda. It was an exciting campaign, and I spent many hours phone-banking, sending out literature, and doing everything I could to help her candidacy.

Ann won the election, becoming the first woman to reach that level of statewide office in Texas in fifty years. The records show what an excellent job she did as State Treasurer. We were delighted by the number of women and minorities she brought into her department.

When she decided to campaign for governor in the election of 1990, I was delighted to be in one of the small focus groups she met with to talk about her campaign. It was critical for Ann to be able to raise "early money," and she had some genuine concerns about women's abilities to give politically.

Most women, no matter what their financial position, usually wrote a check for twenty-five dollars. She knew that she could not be successful unless this habit was changed.

Ann was looking for creative ways to communicate her message to women that if they wanted to support her candidacy they would have to give larger sums. She even said that if women would just add up the cost of the clothing they were wearing at any given time and write a check for that amount she would have the funds she needed.

I came away from the meeting thinking about what I could do to help this remarkable woman become the next governor of Texas. I came up with the idea of starting an organization called "Ann's Fans." I told one of my Caucus friends, Pat Smothers, about the idea.

We worked on the concept of having a photograph of the top part of Ann's face printed on cardboard alongside a genuine Ann's Fan Club card. For $100, an Ann's Fan Club member received this material, in addition to a wooden tongue depressor to use for a handle when she cut out the photo to make her own Ann's Fan. Each member was free to decorate her fan in any way she chose.

Even though it was a fun-filled, wacky idea, the concept caught on and $100 checks started arriving. It became a prestigious symbol to be a member of Ann's Fan Club. We had the fans available for sale at every gathering of women's organizations. At one event, we sold seventeen Ann's Fan memberships in twenty minutes.

Toward the end of the campaign, she told me that on one of her visits she had been in a small coastal city where some woman came up to her to say, "I have an idea for an Ann's Fan Club." Ann told her that such a club had been in existence for some time, raising money for her campaign. Perhaps one difference between that woman and me was that I networked immediately to implement the idea. Thinking about doing something is one step, but carrying it out is another.

I had told Ann early on that we would raise money with Ann's Fans and that, somehow, somewhere, I was going to place a picture of Ann with her fans in a national magazine. The night before the election, Ann was to be in San Antonio for a final appearance. I knew that if I were to carry through with my promise this was my only chance. I called a photographer, Roberta Barnes, whom I had befriended when she first came to San Antonio, to tell her of my plan. I told her that I would have a group of Ann's Fan Club members with their fans at election headquarters in San Antonio that night. I knew that the place would be a madhouse and that Roberta would have just a few seconds to take her photos.

And that is exactly how it happened. In front of the podium, I gathered Ann's Fans and gave them instructions to put their fans in front of their faces when Ann entered the front of the hall. As she came through the crowd, she saw a glimpse of the group with her face on their fans, and she let out a delightful "Whoop." I shouted to her, "Quick, Ann, kneel down in front of the group to let us take a photo." Roberta was busy snapping away, while the whole room was a sea of shouting, pushing, and excited humanity.

Then I told Roberta to call *Time* magazine and tell them about the photos we had. They announced that they had their own photographer traveling with Ann but that they would look at Roberta's photographs. Can you imagine my delight when the next issue of *Time,* the November 15, 1990, edition, carried, on page thirty-four, the picture of Ann and her fans!

To me, this was another amazing example of what happens when people become totally tuned in to who they are. It gives them the courage (audacity) to take an action that, on the surface, might be seen by others as a totally wild and unattainable goal. It's called having the courage of your convictions and then making it happen.

Some time later, I was on a podium with Ann in Austin as a member of the Statewide Steering Committee for Women's Legislative Days. Our governor was giving a greeting to the assembled group, about one thousand people in the ballroom of a hotel. She was paying tribute to the members of the Steering Committee when, much to my surprise, I heard her relating the story of Ann's Fans and the photo in *Time* magazine. I felt enormous pleasure at her words of praise.

I'll never forget how she ended this tribute. She said, "Old Ginger Purdy is someone you can count on. If she says she's going to do something, she does it." The idea that our governor, as busy as she was, would have remembered my small effort and would have taken the occasion of such a public gathering to tell people about it affirmed in my mind what a remarkably generous woman she is. I would not have a moment's hesitation firing up Ann's Fans nationally if she decides to campaign for the Presidency!

Chapter 31
"W6"—Bound With Butter

It is my firm belief that every woman who sets out on a mission to help other women needs as much support as possible. Even though it's been many years since women have started speaking out for themselves, we still have many obstacles in our path that make it extremely difficult.

One of the first lessons I learned back in the eighties—when I made the commitment to make networking work in my life—was that it is critical to know who is "with you." My mentor, Alina Novak, made it clear that networking was the serious business of getting together to get ahead and that it was absolutely necessary to know who supported you. She said that generally if people weren't "with you" they were "against you." Human nature, being as strange as it is, produces many people who want to hear only such negative tales as "Woe is me! Ain't it awful!" They seem to delight in hearing about all the downers you go through.

Fortunately, there are those rare individuals who are true friends and delight in knowing what is positive that happens to you. Alina gave the example of someone calling a so-called friend to tell her some extremely happy news. She said that if there was a silence at the other end of the line, and then you heard the phrase, "Oh, really," that person was not with you. True friends and supporters are delighted to hear of your good fortune.

Any woman who is trying to develop herself to her full potential must be aware of who is with her and who is against her. How many times have we heard that lament, "I thought she was my friend, but she stabbed me in the back and I lost the promotion."

Yes, networking is the serious business of getting together to get ahead. True networkers share and are always willing to help. Those who are out strictly for themselves cannot be counted on to protect you. They are not really networkers. I call them "prospectors." Take my advice, give these gals a wide berth!

I have been both blessed and cursed to come from a large city that has always operated as a small town. Those in power who controlled everything in my city were a small group of white males. If we were not in the inner circle, there was no way we could have a place at the table in anything that had to do with civic and political affairs of the city.

I can remember my friend, author Celia Morris, questioning the great Civil Rights Commissioner Mary Berry about power. "Why," Celia asked Mary, "did women not get the vote when Black men were given the vote with the Fourteenth Amendment?" Celia remarked that Mary looked at her with a generous amount of pity for her naivete to say, "Celia, don't you know that no one ever gives power away? The only way to be powerful is to become so strong that you can demand it."

Closer to home, I have had wonderful support from large groups of women. As necessary as this is, it is imperative to have a small group that you can count on, such as my "W6" Group. We are six women who have been active in local community work and we meet for a monthly breakfast. It is a small sharing group in which we catch up on the news about what is taking place in the city. Because the group is based on trust and respect, and because we are all of one mind when it comes to supporting women in our city, it has a special feeling to it.

We have a great time together and laugh frequently; however, we are aware that sometimes we take ourselves too seriously. We know the benefit of the freedom that children get through play. Busy women that we are, we must not forget to play. Therefore, when we first started meeting several years ago, it was my idea to use a fun ritual to increase the bond of friendship we shared.

Remembering how young boys seal their friendship with a blood oath, I proposed an adult female version. At one of our early meetings, I passed around a plate of butter squares. Each woman touched the butter with her index finger. Then we all touched our fingers together until we were bound in butter! We knew, as women, that butter was a great binder in baking, so it seemed appropriate that this method of binding ourselves together was the right ritual for this type of support group. It was a hilarious moment with screams of laughter.

But actually it worked just like the little boys' childhood ritual. We are bound in our desire to do everything we can in our community to see that women receive fair treatment. We are organized, we do strategize, and we know what's happening. And even though we are all very busy now and have not been able to meet recently, we each know that support is there when we need it, just a phone call away.

I only wish that every woman had such a group she could count on for support.

Chapter 32
Networking with International Women

Meeting Cory Aquino, the President of the Philippines, was one of the real thrills of my life. I would never have had the opportunity if not for my membership in the International Women's Forum. In fact, since I was invited to join this select group several years ago, I've met some of the most amazing women in the world: from Wilma Mankiller, Chief of the Cherokees, and Jackie Joyner-Kersee, one of the greatest women athletes of the world, to Violeta Chamorro, President of Nicaragua, to name only a few.

The International Women's Forum was founded in 1982 to create opportunities among women of achievement for the exchange of ideas, experiences, and resources, and to enable members to reach greater heights of excellence in their leadership responsibilities. The organization offers the opportunity to meet with other prominent women throughout the United States and the world. I was honored in May of 1989 to be nominated for membership in this extraordinary organization.

As a long-time women's advocate in my state, I was glad to know that the International Women's Forum recognized that women today have power and responsibility in the major segments of our society, and it should be used—in partnership with men—to address problems in the public and private realm. The IWF has two annual events for its members to meet and get acquainted, the annual conference and gala, and the spring retreat.

I have been able to attend several of these events and it is one of the most exhilarating feelings imaginable to meet women leaders from all over the world. Even more thrilling is the opportunity to share ideas, knowledge, and experiences. It always comes as a pleasant surprise to me at these events to recall that I had always considered myself a follower (the old late-bloomer) and now I network with women worldwide. What an unbelievable change has come over my life! This just reinforces my belief that when one dares to take a risk of self-discovery, dares to use the talents that are uniquely one's own ... amazing things happen.

The opportunity to meet the courageous woman who was then the President of the Philippines was one that I could not pass up. Cory Aquino was on her way back to the Philippines after a meeting in Washington, D.C., with President Reagan. She had expressed a desire to meet with Texas women, so some 250 members of IWF from throughout the state gathered in Dallas for this exciting occasion. Sixteen of us from San Antonio flew up that morning, met for lunch, then flew back in the evening. It was a short trip but one that was long on inspiration.

We met at an elegant hotel and had time before the lunch to network with our Forum members from throughout the state. Going through the receiving line I had no idea that someone was photographing us as we met President Aquino, so it was a nice surprise several weeks later to receive a note from the luncheon chair. She sent not only a photograph of me greeting Cory Aquino but also one of me in conversation with my favorite governor, Ann Richards. Both of these photos have been framed and hold a place of distinction on my "I-love-me wall." (That's what we facetiously call the wall in one's office that holds all the plaques, awards, degrees, etc.)

At the luncheon there were all those women—and two men, the U.S. Ambassador to the Philippines and the Philippine Ambassador to the U.S. Part of President Aquino's entourage consisted of several family members, including her daughter. When it came time for President Aquino to speak, this quiet unassuming woman came to the podium and declared, "I am a housewife and I want to tell you how we cleaned the house in the Philippines."

I am one of those women's advocates who have always held that we do not have to be ashamed of our femininity no matter what job we undertake. However, I never thought in my lifetime that I would hear the president of a country describe their democratically-elected power using the analogy of a housewife. With gentle dignity, she started at the beginning . . .the arrival at the airport where her husband was assassinated almost before her eyes. Then she described how they had to right the wrongs in the country after many years of corruption, using the comparison of cleaning a house room by room. She also told of "the thieves who stole the family heirlooms." The audience was held spellbound by this remarkable woman telling an unbelievably remarkable story.

Cory Aquino's experience in the Philippines showed the world what "people power" can do against oppression. I know in my own mind and heart I will never forget the television scenes that showed tanks being stopped and surrounded by millions of people. To me that shows that the power of people coming together to stop corruption can put to rest the insane notion that war can solve problems. From a woman's point of view, the only thing that war does is kill our sons and daughters. From the perspective of the world's arms merchants, war is big business. What a horrible way to do business.

Since that day in Dallas, I've thought many times about the experience of meeting and hearing Cory Aquino speak. Even though her tenure as president was not without horrendous problems (many caused by people she thought were her friends), her words and actions, especially using her feminine mentality, is a lesson in righteousness from which all the world's leaders could benefit. I am so grateful to be a member of the International Women's Forum where I have the opportunity to meet leaders like this great woman.

Chapter 33
The University of Texas at San Antonio's Women's Center

One of the outcomes of being a community activist is that you receive invitations to membership on various boards and commissions. In 1992, I was invited to be a member of the Community Advisory Committee for the College of Social and Behavioral Sciences at the University of Texas at San Antonio. It's always a gratifying learning experience to become involved in these efforts. From my perspective as a women's advocate, I was delighted when the committee was divided into three groups and my group dealt with women's issues.

Drs. Linda Pritchard and Linda Schott had been involved with other faculty members on issues important to women. A proposal had been submitted to the Strategic Planning Committee of the University to create a Center for the Study of Women and Gender. The word came to us that the proposal did not have a very high priority and the prospects for such a center did not look good.

We went into high gear strategizing our approach to the situation. We felt a letter-writing campaign was our best bet, so several of us started making phone calls. Soon we had letters of support from a wide variety of community leaders. We were delighted when the Strategic Planning Committee approved the proposal.

A center such as this is of immeasurable value for our part of the country and for the future of women. With the passage of the North American Free Trade Agreement (NAFTA) among the U.S., Canada, and Mexico, and with the other agreements from Latin America that are sure to follow, having a Center for the Study of Women and Gender will become critically important, with its emphasis on research and development.

Like the disgrace of the lack of research concerning women's health, there is still an unbelievable amount of research to be conducted on women's concerns. The funding for such research needs to be at the same level as that for men's concerns. Since most of the people in positions of authority in academia are males, bringing out the full potential of such a center will not be easy.

This is why this research center in the southwest part of Texas is of special importance, here and now — in a state with increasing importance in global markets.

I am keeping my dream alive that this center will be the most vitally significant of any in the hemisphere.

Chapter 34
Networking in Mexico

By 1989, I was well known as a women's advocate in San Antonio, and my favorite example of this "fame" appeared in the *San Antonio Light* newspaper. My friend and colleague Mary Lance had used the incident as the lead in a story on my networking experience. This is what she wrote:

> Last spring, a San Antonio newcomer leafed through the Yellow Pages of the local phone book to find listings for women's organizations. Under the heading of women, she found listings only for women's apparel. Still curious, this businesswoman called directory assistance. "Ma'am," said a youthful man's voice, "there are some white page listings but I don't know what organizations you'd like specifically. Instead, I'd recommend one woman in town who is plugged into everyone and everything about women. Call Ginger Purdy." No greater compliment could be paid to the mother of networking for women than having a phone company representative unofficially send her referrals.
>
> So you can see why I was not too surprised to receive a phone call on a summer morning in 1992 from a young

pediatrician from Jalapa, Veracruz, Mexico, Dr. Martha Palencia Avila. She and her husband, who was head of the Social Security System for the State of Veracruz, were in San Antonio for a vacation with their two sons.

Like some of my other callers, Dr. Palencia had been in touch with the Greater San Antonio Chamber of Commerce, the oldest and largest of our many chambers, said she was looking for the name of an active women's advocate, and they referred her to me. She said she wanted most urgently to meet with me, preferably at breakfast the next morning. Though my day was already full, something told me to rearrange my schedule so we could meet. Her English, while heavily accented, was quite good since she and her husband had lived in Colorado for several years.

The next morning I met an attractive, petite young woman who spoke eloquently about her concerns for the women in her part of the world. We talked for over two hours, discovering how much we had in common, both as individuals and as women. I learned that Dr. Palencia had become discouraged in her practice because of having to treat uneducated mothers again and again for the same problems. Some time before our meeting, she had made the decision to stop practicing and enter teaching and research. She knew she had to do this in order to make more of a difference in women's lives.

At the end of our breakfast meeting, Martha had extracted a commitment from me to go to Jalapa in the fall to help her start a networking organization. She would go home and raise the necessary funds to make the trip possible. Since I had already begun networking with women in Mexico — in Monterrey and Guadalajara — I was thrilled to have this new opportunity.

Sure enough, Martha was as good as her word. Late that summer, I received a call telling me that she had indeed secured the financial help she needed to fund a seminar on how to start a networking group in Jalapa. She had the support to bring not only me but two other colleagues from my Network Power/Texas board. I immediately called Dollie

Bodin and Pat Jasso with a question, "Want to go to Veracruz with me in the fall?" They accepted without delay.

As it turned out, I was already in Mexico when the weekend date for the seminar came around. I was a member of a delegation of San Antonio leaders who accompanied our mayor to Guadalajara for the opening of Casa San Antonio, a trade office to promote the city's business with Mexico. (In fact, I had been to Mexico several times to lobby for the passage of NAFTA. On these trips, I had been able to talk with Mexican women about issues that affected us as women.)

So plans were made for me to fly from Guadalajara to Mexico City where I would meet Dollie and Pat. Martha had made arrangements to have her secretary and a driver pick us up at the airport for the three-hour trip to Jalapa. In the early evening, we arrived at Martha's house where she had prepared a typical Jalapan feast for us. We spent the evening becoming acquainted and going over plans for the seminar. Both groups had prepared agendas and specific outlines for each of us. After dinner, we went to the hotel where the seminar was to be held in order to check out the accommodations.

Dr. Palencia had certainly done her homework in preparing for this event. She had enlisted the aid of a group of her colleagues, all Mexican professional women, including her cousin, Dr. Isabel Bueno, a psychiatrist. The seminar was an invitation-only event limited to fifty attendees.

The next morning, I found the room professionally set up, including a booth at the back of the room for simultaneous dual-translations. It was just like the United Nations! They even had the logos for both of our organizations made into a backdrop for the head table. They had chosen the name "Mujeres en Enlace," which means "women networking together."

The conference tables were set up in a large open square in which we could all make eye contact. It was a thrill for me to see my Mexican professional sisters, whose professions ran the gamut from social worker to dentist, lawyer, and architect.

From the beginning, it was clear that we were all on the

Networking in Mexico

same wavelength concerning women's issues, a fact that I had discovered for myself in my travels in other countries. As in the U.S., we found out that the Mexican women had much in common with each other — more similarities than differences.

What was especially interesting to me was to find out that the Mexican women had the same problem I had in not being able to identify with the extremists at either end of the women's movement. They were "Middle Women" too!

For a day and a half, we shared our experiences about forming a networking organization in an exciting exchange of ideas, questions, and comments. It was probably one of the most exhilarating events in my life. It's amazing how quickly women can bond, in spite of language differences, when they talk about being women. Not only were we sharing information but we were coming to know and respect each other.

I was impressed with the total honesty and trust exhibited among all the attendees at this historic meeting. There was serious business taking place, but in an atmosphere of excitement and fun. There were gales of laughter as I tried to use my broken Spanish, and they used equally broken English. Between Pat Jasso, who is Mexican-American and speaks fluent Spanish, and Drs. Palencia and Bueno, who speak rather good English, we were able to communicate.

The second day was significant for me because of all the attendees who came back, including several new women. At the close of the seminar, we were given speakers' gifts that pleased us greatly! They were magnificent hand-woven Jalapan rebozos or shawls. The Mexican women presented these gifts in boxes covered with photographs of male underwear models — handsome men in Speedo bikinis. It was a fun gesture that we appreciated.

The loveliest aspect of the seminar's ending was when we all met in an outside hall for a reception. There was wine and music and we danced together, doing the traditional dances of that region. What an experience we all shared!

Heading home, we not only left new-found friends but the formation of an organization that today continues helping Mexican women network. Women truly are sisters, and when we share, we move all of us forward to our goal of equality throughout the world.

Chapter 35
Becoming a Full-Time Women's Advocate

Soon after my return from San Diego in 1980 where I had my "Damascus Road experience" combining networking with power, I attended a function called "Women in Focus." It was a reception-type event with a lot of mingling and networking, held in the Officer's Club at Fort Sam Houston. I was still so high from the experience in San Diego that this was a wonderful opportunity to share my enthusiasm for a future networking event in San Antonio.

Margaret Wright, the woman behind the Women in Focus events, played an important part in my early efforts to be a women's advocate. She had a terrific idea to bring women together to focus on what they could do as a group. She single-handedly produced several of these important events for women before the cost became too great for her to continue, but the nourishment that I received from her efforts played an important role in my development. The timing was exactly right for me and my future work. Margaret did go on and get her Ph.D. and I'm sure that today she is still in the business of helping women.

Another woman who had a part in my blossoming as a women's advocate — even though to this day she still doesn't know it — was one of the funniest women I've ever had the pleasure of reading . . . Erma Bombeck. In 1986, when I was the national vice president for membership for WICI, I had written to Erma trying to get her involved in a project. Goodness knows Erma had already done work above and beyond for the organization during the struggle to get the ERA passed. She had since gone on to other things and here I was, trying to get her re-involved in WICI. She wrote me a nice note declining, but there was one sentence that really gave me food for thought: "The Erma Bombeck's of the world have done their work," she said, "now it's time for the Ginger Purdy's of the world to take over." It took me a while to realize that she was exactly right. All I had to do was pump up my self-confidence to the task at hand and then dare to take the risk to do it.

In the ensuing seven or eight years I found myself being drawn more and more into full-time advocacy work. During these years I was an advertising and public relations consultant, which meant that if I wanted to do business I had to drum it up myself. Somehow my heart just wasn't in it when it came to making money.

Understandably, Bob did not take too kindly to this new direction my career was taking me. We had many discussions about my responsibilities as a partner in this marriage to bring money into the common account. It caused me to do no little soul-searching. On the one hand, I had to respect where he was coming from; on the other, I had to respect what was going on inside of me at the deepest level. By this time I knew beyond a shadow of a doubt I had been given a job to do that surely came from a power greater than myself that I choose to call God. (God knows that I could never have accomplished what I have without His/Her help!) In all of my meditative sessions and all of my prayer times, the message I received was always the same: You have a job to do in helping women help each other while helping themselves. There were many times when I felt sorely tried and filled with no little guilt over the direction my life was taking, but somehow I found the courage to carry on with my advocacy work despite all the obstacles placed before me.

I know that in 1975 a man named Bob Purdy was put into

my life who helped plant and nurture the seeds of my advocacy work, and this garden we planted together had a more abundant growth than either of us could have imagined. In fact, it was a lot like Jack and his Beanstalk—it grew beyond my wildest dreams. Like the beanstalk, it kept taking me higher and higher into the world of possibility that, before, I had just dared to dream about: women becoming a power block for good in our country ... in our world.

So against all odds, I kept on with my advocacy work. The thoughts of clients and paying projects went completely by the boards. I knew one thing ... I was happiest when I was doing women's advocacy work. Not only that, I was in my most creative element, and that alone told me that I was on the right track. Like the old saying my grandmother was fond of using, "Where there's a will, there's a way," I knew that somehow I would have the means to carry on this work.

Several years ago, I was invited to address a large national organization holding its conference in a huge convention center. As my hostess led me into the hall where fifteen hundred women were waiting to hear me speak, I laughed to myself. "Could this be the same woman whose fear of public speaking was so great that she could not give her fish-pond booth report to the Wilshire Elementary School PTA?"

I had come a long way! Not only did I feel positive about myself, but I knew that I had a great speech to give. I also had a wonderful, warm, fuzzy feeling inside when I thought about the really large honorarium I was to receive for a twenty-minute speech.

Since starting on my crusade, I have given hundreds of speeches to thousands of women (and some men) in all parts of this country and overseas. I have a file that holds many letters and notes complimenting me on my speaking ability. It is gratifying—knowing where I started and where I am now—to see the progress I've made. I'm not saying that I am the *best* public speaker, but I'm *good* at it.

Several years ago, I traveled to Florida to do several seminars for the Federally Employed Women, Inc. (FEW), Space Coast Chapter. The women who had invited me to speak had heard me give a presentation at the FEW national training program the year before. I was flattered when they called me to say that they just had to have me come to Florida to speak to their group.

I had great success with both of the seminars. Later I received a letter from the woman who had invited me — a letter that has been a true source of affirmation for me. She explained that because of local scheduling conflicts my workshop had been slated as the last session of the day. In public speaking lingo, this is known as the suicide time slot, 3:00 to 4:30 P.M. The women who had been planning their local training program for nine years had tried various methods, speakers, and topics to hold participants in the late afternoon, but without much success. She said that several times over the years she had seen the size of the audience reduced by as much as 50 percent ... until this year. "Both days," she told me, "with an audience in excess of 100 people you were able to hold their attention and keep them actively participating with a loss rate of five percent." The letter ended with these wonderful words: "I knew that Ginger Purdy was truly a remarkable speaker and that I would not hesitate to recommend her to anyone or any group."

Moving from experiencing primal panic as a public speaker to being able to offer a pleasing, professional performance as a speaker let me know just how far I had come. Not only did I like public speaking, but I discovered that I did indeed have a great deal of "ham" in me.

It's wonderful to enjoy doing something like public speaking, knowing that you can do it effectively and that you are paid for it. It just bears out my original premise that if I can do it, anyone can!

Part Eight

Make My Challenge Your Challenge!

Chapter 36
Powerful Women Who Have Touched My Life

While I am grateful to all my brothers and sisters for the lessons of life I've learned, it is the *women* who have proved such a blessing to me, and I have been fortunate to have some of the most powerful women on the national scene cross my path. I have learned from every one of them.

I didn't always understand some of the things women were trying to teach me. I'm thinking back to 1972 when I was a delegate at the National Women's Political Caucus meeting in San Antonio. Gloria Steinem came to speak and there was such a throng of women trying to get in to hear her that although the meeting was moved to a larger room, the place was still packed. I could not even get inside but was standing in a crowd at the middle of one of the doors. When she finished her speech, she asked for questions from the audience. To this day I still don't know how she saw my hand but she singled me out and called on me. My question was: "Is there room in the women's movement for a traditional woman like me?" Her answer: "We're *all* traditional women. We just need to talk together." It took me years to finally understand what she was saying, but that's alright; I came to my understanding when I was suppose to. I believe with all my heart that each individual sees the light of understanding exactly when the time is right for her. There are no mistakes!

So even though I was late coming into the movement for equality for women, when I got the message I really got it. I remember being on a plane sitting next to Sarah Weddington. I had met her earlier through the Texas Women's Political Caucus and had always been in awe of her. What a role in history she has won for herself — what a right she has won for women!

What I've always loved about her is her graciousness and openness with her admirers. On the plane we spent our time talking about women's issues, and Sarah pointed out a fact I had not recognized: When I told her that I had gone to work several weeks after graduation from college in 1948 and had worked continuously ever since, she said I had been a role model for women. What she meant was that most women in my generation earned their Mrs. degrees, as I had, but then opted to be housewives. (I say "housewives," not "working women," because although housework is work, unfortunately to many people it has no value, compared with working outside the home.)

Watching Sarah Weddington address a large group of college students is quite an experience. She holds them spellbound. There's no moving or talking among them; they hang on her every word. The last time I heard her speak was at the University of Texas at San Antonio during Women's History Month in 1994. I was delighted to see so many young men in the audience and to hear their insightful questions.

As I grew in understanding of the women's movement, I was indebted to Betty Friedan for her book that started it all, *The Feminine Mystique.* I was even more in tune with her second book, *The Second Stage,* since it bore out my belief that men and women were different for a reason! Her latest book, *The Fountain of Age,* shows me how critically important it will be for mature, prime-time women to take their place in helping to rule this world. I'm more convinced of their importance in the scheme of things since my return from the United Nation's 4th World Conference on Women in Beijing.

Another of the early feminists who touched my life in the most profound way is Shirley Chisholm. I've told in an earlier chapter what a great influence she had on me. I am indebted to her for making me realize how important it is to organize and strategize to accomplish my goals. Yes, time spent with her changed my life!

I doubt if there is a woman around who doesn't hold Eleanor Roosevelt in highest esteem. She was one of the greatest friends women have ever had. And no matter how many brickbats are being thrown her way, I think of Hillary Clinton as today's Eleanor!

Celia Morris, author and worker for women, gave my advocacy further inspiration when she introduced me to Ellen Malcolm in Washington just as she was starting "Emily's List,"—an acronym for **Early Money Is Like Yeast**, a network of informed women and men committed to contributing early money to Democratic women running for political office. Celia said, "Tomorrow we're going to have breakfast with a woman who has an idea that you will just love. It uses women's symbolism for political purposes." She knew that one of my chief complaints about the procedures of business and politics is that for them to be successful they must be done as men have always done them. I have never wanted to be apologetic about doing anything as a woman! I came back to Texas and started spreading the word about how this great new idea could help elect women to office.

And in my mind, one of the greatest women ever elected to office is former Governor Ann Richards. I have been proud to call her friend since our days in the Texas Women's Political Caucus. If ever a woman helped other women up the ladder of success it is Ann Richards. And, of course, Barbara Jordan has always been right up there at the top of my "sheroes" list! (The morning I had just typed this sentence, Melissa called from Houston to tell me the announcement of Barbara's death had just come over the news wire. I sat there staring at the sentence for a long time. Not only I but the whole world had just lost one of its truest lights.)

In 1980, when we were planning the second Network Power/Texas seminar in San Antonio, my first choice to keynote the event was Barbara Jordan. From the first time I heard her speak, I was totally captivated by this courageous and amazing woman. She had recently returned to Texas from Washington and had started her teaching career at the LBJ School of Public Affairs. I sent the invitation to her with high hopes for an affirmative answer.

Back came a most gracious refusal. Of course I was disappointed but certainly understood her reasons. With a health problem that would restrict her activity, she had chosen to place her resources where they would count the most— teaching the citizens of tomorrow. I have kept her letter all these years. In the spring of 1994 I attended a fund-raiser for Governor Ann Richards in San Antonio at which Barbara Jordan was a guest. I retrieved the letter and took it with me, and when I had a chance to chat with her for a few minutes I showed it to her. She was quick to note it was thirteen years old. She wrote across the bottom of the letter that what she said in 1981 was still true today, dated and signed it . . . and I will cherish it forever. It will be handed down to my granddaughter.

Barbara Jordan truly was one of my "sheroes." She has been an inspiration to so many women by what she has accomplished in her career and what she has said in her speeches.

I hold great fondness in my heart for Liz Carpenter. She came to San Antonio soon after her return from D.C. to speak at the first networking seminar in 1981. She has generously given me networking plugs in her speeches around the state. There is not a more devoted worker for women's causes than this grand lady!

I'm looking at a photograph on the wall behind my desk that

has been there since 1981. (See frontispiece) It is a photo of eight women representing the coalition of women's groups that I got together that started me on my "women's work." The women are coming up over a hill on the street behind my house. We are holding hands and wearing T-shirts that say, "When Women Join Hands All Things Are Possible." I believe that statement with all my heart! It is the hope that has kept me going all these years.

That hope has been borne out by what I saw in China! During three weeks at the United Nation's 4th World Conference on Women in the fall of 1995 I saw it happening with my own eyes! I believe that women are joining hands all over the world. They will no longer let minor differences keep them apart. "Human rights are women's rights." That is the uniting message that came out of that truly incredible gathering of women.

The women that I met in China, like the other powerful women who have touched my life, have empowered me to speak up and out!

Chapter 37
Follow Me to Freedom!

Late as I was in finding my place in the women's movement, I'm grateful that I kept on until I found it! And I did bloom where I was planted. With that flowering I came to experience what it feels like when a woman realizes her worth as a human being. It gives her the courage to stand up for her rights. Once that happens she is never the same again. She loses the fear that has dominated much of her life. She is free. Now she can act!

And how did I act? In December of 1991, on a beautiful sunny beach in San Juan, Puerto Rico, I put pen to paper to write about a movement that could free the majority of women in this country to take charge of their own lives. It would allow them to be in control of their lives without going against their most cherished ideals or those of their partners. They could embrace this philosophy which would allow them to be who they really were without sacrificing anything that they loved as women.

I remember the excitement I felt when my late, good friend sociologist Alice Frankze introduced me to the precept behind the Beyond War movement. About the only part I played in Alice's work with that organization was helping her set up a meeting at my church.

After spending those three weeks in China in the fall of

1995 for the United Nation's 4th World Conference on Women, I came back convinced that our movement for equality is not only unstoppable but accelerating daily.

Five days after my return from Beijing I was in Atlanta for the fall conference of the International Women's Forum. There I heard Secretary of Health and Human Services Donna Shalala report on the conference and her assessment of the state of the women's movement. She calls it, "the maturing of the women's movement." I agree with her 100 per cent! We both witnessed a first for the world: women uniting behind a cause as never before. They are presenting a united front on human rights as women's rights, and women's rights as human rights.

Next I was off to Kansas City for WICI's National Professional Conference. These were three trips within a short time frame, one of them very long, and I learned something about jet lag that I didn't know: You count one day of jet lag for each time zone you go through. Well, I had been going through a lot of them in the past month, never realizing I was experiencing a king-size case of jet lag.

Driving to a speaking engagement a couple of days after my return from China, I stopped for a red light and happened to glance down at the bottom of my black dress. The hem appeared to be out a bit. I drove on. At the next stop light I noticed my left sleeve. Funny, I thought, I never noticed that rather rough edge. Then I glance at the right sleeve, same thing. All of a sudden it hit me: I had my dress on inside out! Quickly I turned into the first driveway — it was the Bonanza Steak House — and sheepishly told the waitress my problem, much to her amusement, then darted into the restroom to change. Back in the car I sat for a while until I calmed down, then said a little prayer of thanks that I had discovered my predicament before facing the audience. That incident has certainly made me have more respect for jet lag!

What motivated me to go to Beijing? It was listening to that same old still, small voice inside of me — which was no small matter since it has taken almost half my life to pay close attention to it. I was always too busy listening to others and trying to please them.

In October of 1994, returning to San Antonio from a conference in Dallas where I had been with a long-time friend and colleague who was then living in Beijing, it surprised even me when I suddenly announced that next year I was going to China for the women's conference. A week later, when my daughter Melissa called from Houston to say that her paper was sending her to China next year to cover the women's conference, I knew that small voice was right. I was supposed to go to China. God had plans for me there. And God, in graciousness, was letting me have a daughter there, too!

I traveled with a group of forty women. Most were members of the National Institute for Leadership Development. They were college presidents, professors, administrators, and counselors. It was a compatible, fun-loving group. Since we were observers at the NGO (non-government organizations) conference, the Chinese sent us out to a resort town called Huairou which was about an hour and a half from Beijing where the United Nations Conference took place. Melissa was in a five-star hotel in Beijing. Our hotel had no stars; in fact, the accommodations were pretty dismal. We decided that the place must have been closed up for years because when we opened the door to our room the stench of mildew was almost overpowering. My roommate discovered that if we put Neosporin under our noses it took the mildew smell away and we could go to sleep. After we got into the conference proper, we were so tired at night we had no trouble sleeping.

The first few days were pretty hectic. Not only were we far from Beijing, but *our* group was even farther out—our hotel was another twenty minutes from the conference site, so we were at the mercy of the bus system which took several days to get on some kind of schedule. The Chinese security was very tight and heavy-handed at first. I believe they were simply overwhelmed by the sheer numbers they had to deal with. After all, it was the largest conference—40,000 to 50,000 people—ever in the history of the world!

Eventually things calmed down. It was extremely difficult

to find the events one wanted to attend. Since there were some five thousand seminars, workshops, etc., one was on overload most of the time. The conference site covered more than a hundred acres so there was a lot of walking!

The weather at first was very hot; then it started raining and it kept on raining. At one point, TV showed 20,000 umbrellas, under each a woman waiting to get into a building that seated 1,500. They waited in a downpour for over an hour trying to get inside to hear Hillary Clinton speak. I was one of those women. I got to within a foot of the door when a line of Chinese security men pushed us all back. There could have been a disaster of major proportions if someone had fallen on the stairs but thankfully that did not happen. As we waited, we talked about America's First Lady. Many of the women from other parts of the world questioned us about why Hillary Clinton gets such bad press in our country. They all think that she is wonderful, especially for the work she has done for the last twenty years for the Children's Defense Fund. Our answer: There are too many men in our country who are afraid of a woman who is assertive and intelligent!

Plowing through all the water led one woman to remark that Huairou was the "Woodstock of the women's movement"! What was amazing to me was that no one minded the weather. We were all too busy meeting and getting to know each other. We did not want to lose a minute of the precious time we had together. The women were just incredible. They were the most friendly, loving, and spirit-filled women I have ever been with. There was a man at our hotel from an African country. One morning at breakfast one of our members asked him why he was there. He said, "I am here for my mother, my wife, and my daughter."

I've said that next to the birth of my daughters, my time in China was the most incredible experience of my life. The things I saw and heard really made an impact on me. It made me more sure than ever that what I am doing with my life as an advocate for women is right.

There are several things I experienced at Huairou that I'll

never forget. One is the brave women lawyers of Nepal. Their seminar demonstrated how they use street drama to reach the illiterate women in their country and make them aware that a man taking a second wife is breaking the law. In Nepal they use professional actors but they could not get the funding to bring them to China so the lawyers played the roles themselves. It was heart-breaking to see the abuse women go through played out before our eyes, and even sadder to learn how the legal system operates to the detriment of women by taking years for cases to go through the courts since only two women's cases are heard each month. The most horrifying news was how men get rid of disabled or unwanted wives ... they break their legs. Since there is no one to take care of them, they usually die.

One afternoon as my group gathered on the steps of the plenary session building to make plans for our evening meal together, we observed a group of women from Iran getting ready to demonstrate. They had made signs and had posters of the women martyrs who had been killed in their country for doing such things as driving a car or going without their chadors (coverings from head to foot). They had gathered around a cardboard box and were slowly encircling it. I told my roommate, "There is something inside that box. I can see something moving even though there is some blue plastic covering it." The women circling the box were throwing wadded up pieces of paper in it. Then they announced that they were giving a demonstration of how a woman is stoned to death in their country. They cautioned people to throw only small "stones," because — to my horror — I realized there really was a woman in the box! They explained that with small stones the death would take longer and the woman would suffer more. I had nightmares about what I had seen. It is hard to believe that this kind of violence against women is still going on in the world. It was gratifying to hear a Muslim woman say that when this kind of violence is condoned by governments, culture, and religion, those entities have to go!

166   PART EIGHT: Make My Challenge Your Challenge!

A truly incredible experience happened to me at the conference. For the last several years I have given up my clients to spend all of my time as an advocate for women and children. In this work I travel all over, giving lectures and workshops. Most of them concern improving one's self-esteem and sense of self-worth. I look on this as a mission I have with women to help them empower themselves to change their lives and those of their children for the better.

When I saw a seminar listed in our program called "Empowering Women," to be presented by the San Diego Commission on the Status of Women, I knew I had to be there. My roommate and I finally found the location (a classroom on the second floor of the elementary school) and were dismayed to see that the place was already full. The room had a capacity of fifty but there had to be a hundred already jammed in. We squeezed into the back and waited. It was very hot with all the people crowded together. A woman in front of me turned around and said, "Why, Ginger Purdy, what are you doing here?" It was Sue Hamby from Temple, Texas! I had to go half way around the world and meet someone from my own backyard! As we chatted, she reminded me that I had given a seminar in her town many years before. We had not seen each other for almost ten years.

We waited for the seminar to begin. Finally a woman stuck her head in the door and said, "I hate to tell you this but I don't think this seminar is going to make. I believe the San Diego group is one of those who could not get their visas." (It has been noted that some 10,000 people in the U.S. could not get visas, and many seminars did not make for this reason.) A groan of disappointment went up in the room.

At that point, Sue Hamby jumped up and said, "We have Ginger Purdy here, she can do a seminar on empowering women!" And I did! No notes, just the gut feeling that this was what I was supposed to do. There were so many people crowded into that room that I could not even get to the front but had to go out into the hall and back in the front door where even more people were trying to get in. The whole time I was walking I was praying, "Dear God, please let me be a channel for your will."

My roommate said that once we got out in the hall she never could get back into the room. There had to be dozens of people jammed in each doorway. I've never seen so many women (there were some men, too) wanting to find out how to empower themselves. They were from many different countries. I noticed that there were a lot of Japanese women. Many spoke English, some did not. We all agreed that we would help each other translate and that if I spoke too rapidly they would hold up their hands and say, "Stop, Ginger." Then when we were sure everyone understood, I would go on.

I said I was going to tell them how I had empowered myself and how I was now spending all my time teaching women how to do that for themselves. Every once in a while a hand would go up and someone would say, "Stop, Ginger, what's a coalition?" or something else they did not understand. Then I would go on.

I talked for about thirty-five minutes, becoming dry of mouth and uncomfortable because of the intense heat. Finally, I put my hand to my throat and said, "I'm sorry, but I don't think I can go on." Suddenly, from my right, a beautiful black arm shot out of the crowd holding a full bottle of cold water. With that help I was able to finish.

I asked if there were people there who could tell us how they, too, had empowered themselves. The woman who had given me the water was from Detroit. She said she had been a homeless person and that someone had helped her change her life. Now she headed an organization that helped find homes for the homeless.

Several others shared their stories and then it was time to leave. Many came up to thank me and shake my hand. Most gave me hugs. We exchanged business cards and took photos. Many asked if I would come to their countries and talk. My answer was, "God willing." Then it happened. A tiny Japanese woman (she could not have been more than four feet tall) came up to me and took both of my hands in hers. She looked up into my eyes and said, "You have changed my life."

As I told my Mom when I got home, "God sent me to China to reach that one woman and only God knows what she might do with her life when she gets back to her country." I will never forget that special moment when that woman held my hands.

Since then I've had many occasions to share what happened to me in China. I know that as we empower each other we will see miracles happening in our lives and the world!

Another seminar I attended that had an impact on my life was one presented by a coalition of Australian women's organizations entitled, "Women in Politics: Decision-Making for the 21st Century." A banner was hung reading, "Women's Suffrage Centennial, South Australia, 1894–1994." The group had produced a documentary, "Every Woman's Guide for Getting into Politics." The seminar was very well organized with many practical ideas for getting women involved. The presenter's advice was, "Just do it." She said, "Don't wait for the light at the end of the tunnel, get down there and light the bloody thing yourself!"

We broke into small groups to brainstorm ways of getting women politically involved. In my group there was a Nigerian politician whose country was mostly under military rule, a Japanese teacher, a trade union official from Denmark, and a woman from the Cook Islands where there has never been a woman in parliament. We were later joined by political activists from Illinois and Israel.

Our group's brainstorming brought forth the need for a global network of political woman and an international Emily's List. It was an educational experience for me to be with such fascinating women, many of whom held important political positions in their countries. We had much to share and I was impressed with how considerate everyone was to make sure that all had a chance to participate. Our main question was, "How can we take the one issue that binds all of us together — worldwide violence aginst women and girls — and use it in the political arena?"

I later sat in a classroom with a small group of women waiting for a seminar, "Not at the Table, Women as Economic Decision-Makers," that did not make. No matter. When women gather we still make things happen. As we sat talking, a beautiful black woman told us a delightful story. It seems Aunt Esther had fallen and broken her hip. Outside the emergency room the woman's niece was waiting and chatting with another young woman who said she was waiting for news about her aunt who had also fallen and broken her hip. It soon became evident that the two women were talking about the same aunt. The beautiful ending? One woman was white, the other black. It proves what women have always known: Love knows no color.

Yes, my experience in China was life-changing. It let me see the big picture of women's long struggle for equality as I had never seen it before. In the journal I kept the three weeks I was there is this notation dated September 5, 1995:

> This just popped into my head, the last chapter in my book should be, "Come on in, There's Room for All of Us!" Bejing is going to have a lasting impact on women politically!

When I got home, I realized it should not just be the title of the last chapter but of the entire book!

On the plane coming back we shared stories. One of the more delightful ones I heard was the advice an illiterate Nigerian grandmother gave to her granddaughter as she prepared to go to Beijing:

1. There is nothing that is hard that eventually

doesn't get soft.
2. There is nothing inside men's trousers that is more important than what is inside a woman's head.
3. When people ask where you are from, say, "Don't ask me where I'm from because for now I am here." And
4. I have a right to be here, there, and everywhere!

This grandmother didn't even know where Beijing was but her advice to her granddaughter showed that she was wise in the ways of the world.

There are other wise women who have recently touched my life because of this world gathering of women. One is Kittu Riddle, now of San Antonio but who lived and taught in China. A Ph.D. in Home Ecomomics who is busier than ever in retirement, publishing "Storyletters"— women's stories to be read, retold, enjoyed, shared, discussed, wondered at, and respected ... stories which help us to see our commonalities and celebrate our diversities. These are real stories of women who have lived or are living. In just a few years Kittu's publications are now worldwide, empowering women and creating our very own "Herstory."

To Dr. Ruth Burgos-Sasscer, the first woman president of San Antonio College, I owe a tremendous debt of gratitude because it was through her efforts that I was able to join her China-bound group. Maria Berriozabal, the former San Antonio City councilwoman and mayoral candidate, was a member of the U.S. delegation to the conference and a long-time San Antonio worker for women whose "Hispanas Unidas" is empowering many Latina women. I feel honored to know this brilliant woman and am pleased to see her growing influence on a global level. Patricia Castillo is another San Antonio woman who was in China and is a leading advocate to stop violence against women through her work with the Benedictine Resource Center. I had admired Pat from afar and now I call her friend and colleague.

I call us "The Beijing Four," and the events we planned together both before and after the Beijing conference have bound us together in a very special way. In fact, we're already talking about going to the next conference in the year 2000!

> Your proper concern is alone the action of duty, not the fruits of the action. Cast away all desire and fear for the fruits and perform your duty.
> *The Bhagavad-Gita*

Duty! So there it is, the story of one woman's journey from the depths of victimhood to the exhilarating height of freedom. All through the caring of others who helped her learn to love herself, gave her the courage to speak up and the desire (and duty!) to go out and help others do the same. There are thousands of you out there that are my story. We have been the silent majority but we can no longer remain mute. We must speak up and out for the sake of our children, for those who come after us, for the future of the world. The ills that are plaguing our world cannot be solved by men alone. The talents of women are desperately needed. Women can no longer ignore their duty. They must become politically active. That is the only solution to poverty and the other ills that keep women from equality.

Just as I have dared to go public with my story, tell yours, tell all your sisters. By going to the voting booth and speaking with one voice we can make the miracle of our own freedom happen. So yes, tell all your sisters to "come on in, there's room for us all!"

Coda

Because networking has played such an important part in my life as I developed those leadership characteristics necessary for my work as a woman's advocate, I have spent many hours thinking about the women I've networked with these last fifteen years. After all, one doesn't get called the "Mother of Networking" in her part of the country for taking the subject lightly! So I started putting down names, thinking, what if I leave someone out? What if this, what if that? In the final analysis I rightly thought: These women have all played a part in getting me to the point I am at today, so go ahead and write about them.

And of course I have to start with my family, even though I've had their love and support longer than fifteen years. My truly incredible ninety-one-year-old Mom is my window on the world. She keeps me informed about everything that's happening. And my only sister, Joanie, a now-retired but busy golfer who spent twenty-something years as a full-time housewife and mother of five, then had a career as a children's buyer. She has always astonished me with the things she could do—from handling an electric drill to making auto repairs. Long-time friends like Camille Becker, June Daniels, June's daughter Deborah, and Peggy Peterson have been my most loyal cheering section. And of course all of my daughters fall into this "incredible" classification.

There are so many women who have touched my life with their friendship, love, and support. The women who have helped me run Network Power/Texas all these years are a very special group. They are all kindred spirits, bound together in our mission of "women helping women to succeed:" Susan Cameron, our CPA-treasurer whose calming presence has been such a blessing to me, and she's kept us in the black! Annette Bendele, a great ideas person and our own resident interior decorator. Anita Heim, nurse and confidant, the dearest and truest friend anyone could ever have! . . . and she has been just that for me ever since the Women's Chamber of Commerce got started. Rhonda Spurlock Dahlke, a little dynamo who is always willing to give and get for our cause. Katherine Diver, our secretary, so young and yet such a pro at doing community service. Patt Peaslee, a spirit-filled woman who taught me to be aware of "energy vampires." (Those are the women who want you to listen to their sad tale of woe over and over, never intending to get off their "pity pots" and do something useful with their lives. All they want is someone to help them continue with their sickness. They are bad news and if you let them they will drain your energy!) Talya Norman, who showed us all amazing grace during the time her son was fighting a losing battle with brain cancer. Connie Smith, whose goodness and great love for others and great faith have been a blessing to all of us. And then there is Irma Hereford, our newest board member, an emerging star, still a little hesitant but getting ready to really glitter!

Along with glitter there has to be glue to hold everything together. I couldn't have made it all these years without Esther Shuler, the keeper of our database, who was always willing to give above and beyond. We got an added bonus with her husband Rick, certainly the world's best-natured go-fer! Sofie Lim and Wanda Rohm were there from the start always ready to help. For all these women and one very supportive man, I am very grateful.

My WICI colleagues have certainly had a hand in shaping my life as a woman's advocate.

I look back with such fond memories of the WICI conferences, board meetings, seminars, and fun times we've had together. There was Carol Zennie of Dayton, Ohio, my favorite roommate while on the national board and a real whiz at finding shoe bargains! Jane Brust of Houston, whom I met while I was a regional vice president and she was president of the student chapter at Texas A&M. Jane went on to become a top communications pro at M.D. Anderson Hospital and the mother of a beautiful little girl. Cathy Frank, also from Houston, has always been one of my best WICI-sister boosters.

On the international level, Lucy Hobgood Brown, now of Beijing, has always added excitement to my life with her wonderful and humorous newsletters that relate her experiences in the Orient. Her younger sister, Suzie Phillips, closer to home in New Braunfels (thirty miles from San Antonio) has given me a boost with her delightful, high-energy personality and her determination to start a WICI chapter in her small town.

My San Antonio WICI colleagues have always been a source of support for me. Thelma Ledger and Olivia Burdin are two of my most long-time friends. Dear Lupe Young, who turned to me for advice years ago when her sons were young and she was struggling over her desire to be more active in the organization but knowing she had the responsibility of her family; my advice to her was, "First things first, Lupe. There'll be time for the organization later." And sure enough, there was. I could always count on someone like Marcy Meffert to keep me chuckling with her wacky sense of humor. And when there was a job to be done there were the likes of Barbara Cheaney, Bonnie Flake, Charlene Blohm, Ajay Castro, Barbara Hendricks, Sammye Johnson, Mary Lance, Annette Richardson, and the pro-of-pros, Mary Denman.

Connie Sonnen is a former Network Power/Texas board member and the first charter member of the Women's Chamber whose non-traditional profession as a jet aircraft mechanic at Kelly AFB prepared her well for her retirement years as a tireless volunteer and political candidate, eventually becoming the secretary of a school board. She has always been an inspiration to me, showing that the retirement years are the best yet for helping others and oneself. Another inspiration is Dolores Beccera, who dared to take the risk of changing her life and is now helping young people change theirs for the better through her work with the I Have A Dream Foundation. Connie and Dolores were two of the first women I mentored, along with Pat Jasso and June Esparza. Pat, who calls me "Mother," went on to run for political office. June has written a wonderful workbook for women going back to school later in life like she did to get their college degrees.

When awards are given for bravery I think of Bonnie Reed, a former judge whose courage in calling attention to a bad law that causes harm for women, even at the risk of damaging her career, will be long remembered by everyone who works to put an end to domestic violence. I've called her "San Antonio's Anita Hill," one very courageous woman!

One of the great learning vehicles I've had is my long-time membership in the Women's Political Caucus. That's where I learned the value of teamwork and experienced the joy of fellowship even in the grueling work of putting out huge mailings. There is nothing that beats the thrill of being in the midst of a winning campaign! Tess Giolma and Francille Radmann, along with Jane Macon and Pat Smothers, were early political mentors for me. And no one could beat Wes Hiatt in the political smarts department. For loyalty to a cause there was always Darlene Murnin, Martha Anderson, Laura Burt, Esther Curnutt, Kay Sharp, Ruth Stewart, Welda Smith, Karen Vaught, Paula Starnes, Mary Green, and the ultimate "worker for water," Fay Sinkin.

One of my most memorable Caucus workers was Pat Smother's grandmother, Billie Vaughan. We stuffed envelopes together during Ann Richard's campaign for governor. "Grandma" was then eighty-five. Her life story would certainly make a fabulous book: going from factory-hand to selling eggs and milk during the Depression, practicing nursing during World War II, becoming a schoolteacher, author, political activist, and woman's advocate. I wish we could have cloned Billie!

My town has been fortunate to have such a worthy group

of women judges like Shay Gebhardt, Carmen Kelsey, Mary Roman, Karen Crouch, and Martha Tanner. And city coucilwomen, former and present, like Maria Berriozabal, Helen Ayala, Ruth Jones McClendon, Lynda Billa Burke, and Helen Dutmer who later became the first woman county commissioner. Now we have a woman county judge, Cyndi Taylor Krier, another first.

At the state level I've learned so much from San Antonio state representatives Christine Hernandez, Sylvia Romo, Karyne Jones Conley, and Leticia Van De Putte. These women amaze me with their ability to carry on a political career while many are nuturing families — in Leticia's case a husband and six children in addition to being a pharmacist.

Civic leader and former mayor of San Antonio Lila Cockrell has been a role model for me in the field of community service. I have been fortunate in being able to call on her for advice. And another great San Antonio "civic institution," Amy Freeman Lee, Ph.D. and degrees in nine other disciplines, has been my idol for years. She is truly the wisest woman I've ever known and I could listen to her talk forever. Plus she loves good champagne and is just plain fun to be with.

I have long admired Sister Elizabeth Anne Sueltenfuss, president of Our Lady of the Lake University. She is what I call a real human being and showed her courage and spunk by joining the Women's Chamber at its very beginning. She knew a good thing right off! Divine Providence never steers one wrong!

My Women's Chamber of Commerce colleagues were some of the bravest women in San Antonio, boldly stepping away from the status quo to give women a better chance for success in our city. In that group were Barbara Nelson, Pat London, Mary Ellen O'Neill, Anita Heim, Dora Salinas, Katherine Diver, Diane de los Santos, Brigitte Saidi, and Bridgette Sopper Oliva (who, by the way, took on the presidency while pregnant with her first child, carrying on a full-time law practice, and handling other community commitments.) Elizabeth Lindell, my lawyer and friend, came into my life courtesy of the Women's Chamber where she is a director. Another lawyer, Karen Crouch, also did yeoman work for the Chamber before running a very professional and successful campaign for a judgeship. And speaking of work, I must pay tribute to our office manager, Phyllis Culbert. If ever a person gladly performed her job as a labor of love, it is this woman.

Out in the community I am proud to count as friends such media women as Marina Pisano, who always provided a sympathetic ear to my continual rantings about the unfair treatment of women in the media. To Lynnell Burkett, Veronica Salazar, Maria Elena Torralva Alonzo, Susan Yerkes, Lesli Hicks, and the dean of them all Mildred Whiteaker, I am indebted for all the support they have given my advocacy efforts down through the years. Back in the eighties when I first started out, I once took a press release to Mildred with a diagram of the way I wanted the page to look. Not only did she like it, she used it. When the word got out what I had done, I was something of a heroine for awhile because Mildred was one tough newspaperwoman who did not suffer fools gladly. I just chalked up her actions to her being a great supporter of women. She knew, even then, that this thing called "networking" was going to be a boon to women's progress toward equality.

Other San Antonio women who have touched my life are Mary Q. Kelly, my International Women's Forum roommate, one heck of a smart lawyer even by the good ole boy's standards, and a "shop till you drop shopper" of awesome proportions! Janie Groves, super smart advertising agency owner who knows how to work hard and still have fun, and a great traveling companion. Evelyn Biery, a most gracious hostess, who never failed to offer her magnificent home to nonprofit groups seeking elegant meeting sites. Jo Ann Crow gave generously of her time and talents to supply the slides that enhance my lectures and workshops. And dear, dear Julia Knight, former school principal, who even wrote a song for us, "I'm Glad I Am A Woman," for one of our early celebrations of the vote. Not only did she write the song, she even got her

AKA choir to perform.

Not every woman's advocate is lucky enough to have a retired general say to her, "Ginger, I can't say no to you!" when asked to serve on the first Women's Chamber board, but that's what retired Brigadier General Lillian Dunlap, whom we lovingly call Lil, did for me. A former chief of the Army Nurse Corps, Lil is a five-star in the field of caring. Those tireless YWCA wonders Helen Wronski, Veatrice Williams, and Candi Ramirez, have always impressed me with their dedication to making things better for our city's less fortunate women and children. Candi always makes me feel good just listening to her sunny laugh. And speaking of laughter, there is no one funnier than Nancy Braun whom I've named the "resident comedienne" of the Women's Chamber. I thank my stars to have found her when we were just starting out! Through her hilarious jabs at her sisters, "Self-confidence is putting on lipstick without a mirror!", and looking out at an audience of seven hundred women and students gathered for the Women's Chamber's first Great Treasure Hunt, "My gosh, this looks like a PMS convention!", Nancy lovingly pokes fun at us, reminding us to put more humor in our lives. It's the healthy thing to do.

It's a real miracle to see how enriched my life has become since I became committed to making networking work for me back in the early eighties. Such women as Joyce Coleman, the executive director of the Battered Women's Shelter, who got the position while serving on the Network Power/Texas board and has moved the Shelter forward to be one of the best run in the state, Marie Goforth, the founder of the "I Have A Dream" San Antonio organization, who is also a former member of the Network Power/Texas board, Rosemary Stauber, the founder of the Bexar County Women's Center, Jo Floyd, who is responsible for San Antonio having a Women's Hall of Fame, Kay Ford, who brought together the Women's Coalition, Aaronetta Pierce, who has enriched our city's culture through her work of promoting African and African-American art, and Ruth McLean Bowers, who has always supported women . . . all of these remarkable women have added to the quality of my life.

Some of my most loyal supporters have been women with whom I've gone to church for many years. Women like my neighbor Katy Riggs, a retired Episcopal priest, always a very handy and sympathetic ear, and Laura Frances Davis with whom I started teaching Church School back in the sixties. Nina Huber, Gode Roth, and Frances Richmond were some of the first women I met when I took my three-year-old to preschool classes and found my church home. My backyard neighbor, AB Carson, has been a dedicated social secretary faithfully clipping every photo of me that appears in the newspaper and handing it to me as she goes down the aisle on Sunday.

Another group of "spiritual supporters" has been my reunion group lovingly nicknamed by the restaurant's waitresses as "The Muffin Ladies." Each Saturday morning at eight o'clock we meet for an hour to share what our week has been like from a spiritual point of view. It is always comforting to know that I can rely on Jill Phelps, Cynthia Jones, Margaret Allerkamp, Marise Melson, Phyllis Culbert, and Judy Mercer for unconditional love and support.

Elsewhere in this book I've told of another support group named the "W-6 Group." It was kind of a secret-type thing since we felt that our dear brothers sometimes did not let us in on everything that was happening. These were women from the business and community part of my life, but as warmly supportive as the others. Evelyn Harrison, Pat London, Cindy Taylor, Sara Jackson, and Linda Guerra Matthews kept us up-to-date on what was going on in our town.

I'm sure if one certain woman had not entered my life this book would never have seen the light of day. I met Jan Kilby, Ph.D., at a City-Wide Network Night meeting in the late spring of 1993. I remember that she introduced herself as a teacher and writing consultant. We went our separate ways but soon something very strange started happening to me. Now, I had been in the process of writing this book for over ten years.

In the last year I had really gotten down to the business of getting it finished. My daughter Martha had spent an entire summer helping me with the task, but I was still at cross-purposes on how to put it all together. Suddenly Jan's name started popping up in my mind at random times. At first I paid no attention to it, after all I had barely met the woman. Then it kept happening with such frequency that I knew I was supposed to get in touch with her. When I called her and explained what had been happening to me I hoped she wouldn't think I was some sort of kook and hang up. Thankfully she heard me out and agreed to meet with me the following Saturday. After talking for several hours she agreed to help me organize the book. And organize she did. She has truly been my "book-borning savior!"

Here clearly was another case of listening to that still, small voice inside that never steers one wrong. When I have failed to heed that inward voice it has led to less than happy times for me. Though few in number, thank goodness, some women have not dealt kindly with me. Sometimes this is hard to take. A talk I heard one time helped me with this. Gaylin Norris, a counselor, said that in every rumor there is a kernel of truth; one must look for it and learn from it. These are important lessons.

I've also heard it said that when we meet someone and there is a feeling of dislike inside of us, it means that we see something in that person that we refuse to see in ourselves. That thought has always given me reason to pause. One of the welcome things I've learned from self-discovery is that it not only uncovers character *defects* but character *assets* of which we have not been aware. Getting to really know oneself and the motives that lead us to do what we do takes honesty and courage. I know that I am a better person for getting on that road to wholeness. I also know I would never have discovered the "real" Ginger if it had not been for networking and all the wonderful women I have met and networked with along the way.

HOW THE WOMEN'S CHAMBER OF COMMERCE STARTED IN SAN ANTONIO, 1988: Left to right: Barbara Hendricks, Peg Murray, Willie Cunningham, Ajay Castro, Alice Franzke, Annette Bendele, Ginger Purdy, Martha Langer, Barb Nelson, Wanda Rohm, Rhonda Spurlock Dahlke, Douglas Clark, and Dollie Bodin.

Works Cited

"Big Mouths, Big Losers." *Time,* 19 November 1990: n.p.

Boston Women's Health Book Collective. *Our Bodies, Our Selves.* New York: Touchstone Books, Simon and Schuster, 1973.

The New Our Bodies, Our Selves. New York: Touchstone Books, Simon and Schuster, 1984.

Caplan, Paula. *The Myth of Women's Masochism.* New York: Dutton, 1985.

Dobbs, Mary Lou. *The Cinderella Salesman.* New York: Farnesworth Publishing Company Inc., 1982.

Foxworth, Jo. *Boss Lady: An Executive Woman Talks About Making It.* New York: Crowell, 1978.

_____. *Wising Up: Mistakes Women Make in Business and How to Avoid Them.* New York: Dell, 1980.

Friedan, Betty. *The Feminine Mystique.* New York: Norton, 1963.

_____. *The Second Stage.* New York: Summit Books, Simon and Schuster, 1981.

Harris, Thomas A. *I'm OK, You're OK.* New York: Avon, 1976 and 1993.

Lance, Mary. "A Network Star: Purdy Tunes Women In to the Power of Contacts." *San Antonio Light,* 8 October 1989, sec. J: n.p.

McDermott, Marise. "On the Necessity of Developing A Women's Chamber of Commerce." *San Antonio Light,* 7 June 1988, sec. E: 7.

Morris, Celia. *Fanny Wright: Rebel in America.* Champaign: University of Illinois Press, 1992.

Peck, M. Scott. *The Road Less Traveled.* New York: S & S Trade [Simon and Schuster], Touchstone Books, 1980 and 1988.

Roddick, Anita. *Body and Soul: Profits With Principles: The Amazing Success Story of Anita Roddick and The Body Shop.* New York: Crown Publishing Books, 1991.

Schweir, Miriam. *Feminism: The Essential Historical Writings on Feminism.* New York: Random House, 1972.

Wallace, Amy. *The Book of Lists.* New York: Bantam, 1977.

Warner, Carolyn, (ed). *The Last Word: A Treasury of Women's Quotes.* Englewood Cliffs: Prentice Hall, 1992.

Index

Index

Adams, Margaret, 42, 75
Al-Anon, 10, 12, 57-58, 96-98
Allerkamp, Margaret, 179
Alonzo, Maria Elena Torralva, 177
American Association of University Women, 72, 83
American Broadcasting Company (ABC), 78-80
Anderson, Martha, 175
Anguiano, Lupe, 54-55
Ann's Fans, 129, 134-37
Aquino, Cory, 141-43
Atwood, Margaret, 43
Australian women's organizations coalition seminar, 168
Ayala, Helen, 176

Baird, Zoe, 49
Barnes, Roberta, 136
Battered Women's Shelter, 178
Beccera Dolores, 175
Becker, Camille, 34, 172
"Beijing Four, The," 171
Bendele, Annette, 173
Benedictine Resource Center, 170
Berriozabal, Maria Antoinetta, 88-89, 170, 176
Berry, Mary, 139
Bexar County Women's Center, 71-72, 120, 178
Bhagavad-Gita, The, 171
Biery, Evelyn, 177
Blake, William, 40
Blohm, Charlene, 174
Bodin, Dollie, 148-50
Body and Soul: Profits with Principles, 130
Body Shop, The, 130
Bombeck, Erma, 151-52
Book of Lists, The, 27
Boss Lady, 112
Boston Women's Health Collective, 122
Bowers, Ruth McLean, 178
Braun, Nancy, 178
Brown, Lucy Hobgood, 174
Brust, Jane, 174
Bueno, Dr. Isabel, 148-49

Bufler, Carole, 72, 83
Burdin, Olivia, 174
Burgos-Sasscer, Dr. Ruth, 170
Burke, Lynda Billa, 176
Burkett, Lynnell, 177
Burt, Laura, 175
Business and Professional Women's group (B&PW), 126-27
Butler, Helen, 72

Cameron, Susan, 173
Caplan, Dr. Paula, 122
Carpenter, Liz, 112, 159
Carson, AB, 179
Castillo, Patricia, 170-71
Castro, Ajay, 174
Center for the Study of Women and Gender, 144-45
Chamorro, Violeta, 141
Cheaney, Barbara, 174
Chisholm, Shirley, 110, 119-21, 130, 158
Cinderella Salesman, The, 92
City-Wide Network Night, 84-85, 99, 179
Clarence Thomas-Anita Hill hearings, 44
Clinton, Hillary, 158, 164
Cockrell, Lila, 95, 176
Coleman, Joyce, 178
Collins, Jean, 71
Community Advisory Committee for the College of Social and Behavioral Sciences, 144
Conley, Karyne Jones, 176
Cook, Dan, 55
Crouch, Karen, 176, 177
Crow, Jo Ann, 177
Culbert, Phyllis, 177, 179
Curnutt, Esther, 175

Dahlke, Rhonda Spurlock, 173
Dallas-Fort Worth Airport, 116-18
"Damascus Road" experience, 71, 151
Daniels, Deborah, 172
Daniels, June, 172
Davis, Laura Frances, 179

Dawson, Jean, 79
"Dear Abby," 112-114
De los Santos, Diane, 176
Denman, Mary, 174
Diekow, Wanda, 81
Dillard's, 35-36
Diver, Katherine, 173, 176
Dobbs, Mary Lou, 92
Dolores B., 87-90
Donahue, Phil, 43
Dugosh, Ms., 20
Dunlap, Brig. Gen. Lillian, 178
Dutmer, Helen, 176

"Emily's List," 158, 168
Employment Network, 54
Equal Rights Amendment, 42, 78, 125, 152
Esparza, June, 175

Fanny Wright: Rebel in America, 42
Federally Employed Women (FEW), 154
Feminine Mystique, The, 157
Feminism: The Essential Historical Writings, 42
Flake, Bonnie, 174
Fletcher, Jack, 18-25, 31, 39, 53
Fletcher-Bohrer, Martha, 30-35, 67-69, 180
Fletcher-Owens, Mary, 22, 33, 51, 67-69
Fletcher-Stoeltje, Melissa, 22-23, 31, 33, 67-69, 75, 159, 163
Floyd, Jo, 178
Ford, Kay, 178
Fort Worth, WICI Celebrity Breakfast, 113
Fountain of Age, The, 157
Foxworth, Jo, 112
Frank, Cathy, 174
Frank Brothers, 20
Frankze, Alice 161
Friedan, Betty, 119, 157
Friends of WICI, 82-83, 129

Gebhardt, Shay, 176
Germany, 94-95, 100

Ginger Purdy and Daughters, 67-69
Giolma, Tess, 173
Goforth, Marie, 178
Goldman, Emma, 42
Good Morning America, 69, 78-80
Green, Mary, 175
Groves, Janie, 177
Guarantee Shoe Company, 22

Hamby, Sue, 166
Harris, Sarah, 65
Harris, Thomas A., 97
Harrison, Evelyn, 179
Heim, Anita, 173, 176
Hendricks, Barbara, 174
Henry, Sister, 37-39
Hereford, Irma, 173
Hernandez, Christine, 176
Hiatt, Wes, 175
Hicks, Lesli, 177
Hill, Anita, 175; *see also* Clarence Thomas-Anita Hill hearings
Hispanas Unidas, 88, 170
Honorary Males, 75
Huber, Nina, 179

I Have a Dream Foundation, 90, 175, 178
I'm OK, You're OK, 97
International Women's Forum, 141-43, 162, 177

Jackson, Sara, 179
Jalapa, Mexico, 147-50
Jasso, Pat, 148-50, 175
Jefferson High School, 20
Johnson, Latrell, 71
Johnson, Sammye, 174
Johnson, Sonya, 42
Jones, Cynthia, 179
Jordan, Barbara, 159-60
Joske's of Texas, 22
Joyner-Kersee, Jackie, 141

Kelley, Mary Q., 177
Kelsey, Carmen, 176
Kilby, Jan, 179-80

Knight, Julia, 177
Koch, Mayor Ed, 63
Krier, Cyndi Taylor, 176

Lance, Mary, 146, 174
Landers, Ann, 113
Lange, Eugene, 90
Last Word, The: A Treasury of Women's Quotes, 75
Leadership Loop training program, 129
Ledger, Thelma, 174
Lee, Amy Freeman, 176
Lim, Sofie, 173
Lindell, Elizabeth, 177
London, Pat, 176, 179
Lorenzo, Ms. Ninfa, 65-66
Lyndon Baines Johnson School for Public Affairs, 110, 159

McDermott, Marise, 130
McLendon, Ruth Jones, 176
Macon, Jane, 175
Malcolm, Ellen, 158
Mankiller, Wilma, 141
Matthews, Linda Guerra, 179
Meffert, Marcy, 174
Melson, Marise, 179
Mercer, Judy, 179
Mexican-American Business and Professional Women's Club, 71
Moore, Kay, 71
Morris, Celia, 42, 139, 158
Mount Holyoke, 120
Moynihan, Senator J. Patrick, 42
Mujeres en Enlace, 148
Murnin, Darlene, 175
Murphy, Charles, 79-80
Myth of Women's Masochism, The, 122

National Association of Negro Business and Professional Women, 71
National Association of Women's Centers, 120
National Committee on Pay Equity, 126

National Institute for Leadership Development, 163
National Organization for Women (NOW), 119
National Women's Political Caucus, 45, 110, 119, 125, 134, 156
Nelson, Barbara, 176
Networking for Success, 85, 128
Network Power, 67, 93
Network Power/Texas, 70-75, 83-86, 112, 114, 120, 122-24, 128-29, 147, 159, 173, 174, 178
Network Power/Texas Scholarship Fund, 85-86, 88
New Our Bodies, Our Selves, The, 123
Norman, Talya, 173
Norris, Gaylin, 180
Norsigan, Judy, 122
North American Free Trade Agreement (NAFTA), 145, 148
Novak, Alina, 5, 70-72, 138

Oliva, Bridgette Sopper, 176
O'Neill, Mary Ellen, 176
Our Body; Our Selves, 123

Palencia, Dr. Martha Avila, 147-50
Panama, Bishop of, 38
Peaslee, Patt, 173
Peck, Scott, 69
Peterson, Peggy, 172
Phelps, Jill, 179
Phillips, Suzie, 174
Pierce, Aaronetta, 178
Pisano, Marina, 177
Pritchard, Dr. Linda, 144
Purdy, Robert H., 49-53, 70-73, 79, 94, 122, 152-53

Radmann, Francille, 175
Ramirez, Candi, 178
Rand, Kate Lloyd, 36
Reagan, Maureen, 112
Reagan, President, 78, 126, 142
Reed, Bonnie, 175
Reno, Grandpa, 14

Richards, Ann, "Foreword" by, *ix;* 96, 129, 134-37, 142, 158-59, 175
Richardson, Annette, 174
Richmond, Frances, 179
Riddle, Kittu, 170
Riggs, Katy, 179
Road Less Traveled, The, 69
Roddick, Anita, 130
Rohm, Wanda, 84, 173
Roman, Mary, 176
Romberg, Peggy, 109
Romo, Sylvia, 176
Roosevelt, Eleanor, 158
Roque, Mary Jesse, 71
Roth, Gode, 179

Saidi, Brigitte, 176
St. David's Episcopal Church, 49, 82
Salazar, Veronica, 177
Salinas, Dora, 176
San Antonio College, 71, 87, 170
San Antonio Express-News, 113
San Antonio Light, 130, 146
San Antonio Women's Chamber of Commerce, 128-31, 173, 174, 176, 178
Sanchez, Cessie, 71
Santa Cruz, Dr., 30
Schlafly, Phyllis, 126
Schott, Dr. Linda, 144
Sears, 22
Second Stage, The, 119, 157
Seneca Falls, New York, 42
Shalala, Donna, 162
Sharp, Kay, 175
Shuler, Esther, 173
Shuler, Rick, 173
Sinkin, Fay, 175
Smith, Connie, 173
Smith, Welda, 175
Smothers, Pat, 135, 175
Sonnen, Connie, 174-75
Southwest Texas State University, 109
Southwestern Bell, 129
Stanton, Elizabeth Cady, 42
Starnes, Paula, 175
Statewide Steering Committee for Women's Legislative Days, 136-37

Stauber, Rosemary, 71, 120, 178
Steinem, Gloria, 156
Stewart, Ruth, 175
Stoeltje, Mark, 75
Stoeltje, Melissa, *see* Fletcher-Stoeltje, Melissa
Stoeltje, Sam, 75
"Storyletters," 170
Sueltenfuss, Sister Elizabeth Anne, 176
Symonds, Bonnie Ornelas, 83
Szliak, Roseanna, 72

Tanner, Martha, 176
Taylor, Cindy, 170
TenBoom, Corrie, 15
Texas Family Planning Association, 109
Texas Women's Political Caucus, 41, 44, 157, 158
Texas Women's University (TWU), 17-20
Thomas, Clarence, *see* Clarence Thomas-Anita Hill hearings
Thomas, Marlo, 43
Tillich, Paul, 4
Trinity University, 18-19, 120
Truth, Sojourner, 42
Turner, Suzanne, 60-62

United Nation's 4th World Conference on Women, 157-58, 160-71
University of Texas at San Antonio Women's Center, 144-45

Van Buren, Abigail, 112-114
Van De Putte, Leticia, 176
Vaughan, Billie, 175-76
Vaught, Karen, 175

Warner, Carolyn, 75
Wayne, Claudia, 126
Weddington, Sarah, 157
White, Ben, Jr., (brother), 11, 32-33
White, Ben, Sr. (father), 13, 16-17, 37
White (Taylor), Helen, (aunt), 51
White (Otts), Joanie (sister), 30, 33, 172

White, Mary (mother), 10-15, 31, 32, 37, 39, 122, 168, 172
White, Virginia Nan (Ginger Purdy), 10, 59
Whiteaker, Mildred, 177
Williams, Veatrice, 178
Wilshire Elementary School, 27, 153
Wising Up: Mistakes Women Make in Business and How to Avoid Them, 112
Women in Business, 72
Women in Communications, Inc. (WICI), 44, 60-66, 70-71, 78-79, 82-83, 112-13, 125-27, 152, 162, 173
Women in Focus, 151

Women's Chamber of Commerce of Texas, 128
Women's Legislative Days, 109-11
Women's Lobby Days, 109
Women's Opportunity Workshops, 71, 87
Women's Political Caucus of Bexar County, 43-45, 100
Wright, Margaret, 151
Wronski, Helen, 178

Yerkes, Susan, 177
Young, Lupe, 174
YWCA, 72, 178

Zennie, Carol, 174

About the Author

Ginger Purdy is a native of San Antonio, Texas, dating her ancestry back to the sixteen Canary Island families who founded the city in 1731. A graduate of Texas Women's University, she began her professional career as a fashion artist and has more than 35 years' experience in advertising and public relations.

She has served as an officer on the national and local levels of Women in Communications, Inc., and received her chapter's Headliner Award for outstanding service in 1982. She is founder of Network Power/Texas and the San Antonio Women's Chamber of Commerce. For many years she has been active in the Women's Political Caucus at the local and state levels, and since 1984 has been a member of the State Steering Committee for Women's Legislative Days. During the successful campaign of Ann Richards for governor of Texas, Purdy founded a support group called "Ann's Fans."

Ginger Purdy's mission is women . . . and her advocacy work has taken her all over the United States as well as to Mexico and Germany, and most recently to the United Nation's 4th World Conference on Women in Beijing.

She is the former wife of Dr. Robert H. Purdy, a research scientist, and together they raised five daughters.